Subcontinental Synthesis

Electronic Music at the National Institute of Design, India 1969–1972

T0346747

Edited by Paul Purgas

Subcontinental Synthesis:
Electronic Music at the National Institute of Design, India 1969–1972
Edited by Paul Purgas

First published by Strange Attractor Press 2024
All Texts © The Authors 2024
Design and Layout by Alena Zavarzina

ISBN: 9781913689582

Strange Attractor Press
BM SAP, London,
WC1N 3XX, UK

www.strangeattractor.co.uk

Distributed by The MIT Press, Cambridge, Massachusetts.
And London, England.

Printed and bound in Estonia by Tallinna Raamatutrükikoda.

Contents

Foreword
Budhaditya Chattopadhyay

Sound travels faster than ideas. A sound first impacts directly, in a visceral capacity, connecting bodies, places, environments, and spaces, before it is deciphered on a causal or semantic level. Abstract sounds without immediate cultural associations travel alone, often without a listener, in settings that still need to be initiated. That is why early synthesized sounds, in the 60s, did not have much cultural penetration—although such technologically mediated sounds came in a long line of other media technological interventions into cultural life, such as radio, photography, sound recording, and cinematography. These technologies travelled from the West to the Indian subcontinent via colonial routes for trade and to find broader markets. However, often they were culturally appropriated and assimilated within the complex settings of the subcontinent. They did not remain foreign. These one-way technological transmissions, like the railways and the cinema, were reclaimed as the subcontinent's own, on its terms. It might seem like a miracle that a novel Moog synthesizer travelled to the distant shores of Ahmedabad in 1969, seeking a cultural root in the subcontinent. However, it was, again, in the same lineage of Western technologies travelling to non-Western countries in order to expand their scope and modernist impact. In the 60s, the Indian subcontinent had been saturated with traditional music and culture-specific sounds, and the abstract palette of the Moog synthesizer might have struggled to emplace itself.

← Rabindranath Tagore making an early voice recording, 1921.

On the other hand, the 60s was when many parts of the globe were galvanized with new hope after the end of two World Wars and the decolonization of the Global Souths. The world was ready to experiment with the future. So-called experimental music, e.g., musique concrète, reached a public life during this time, aligned with the technological affordances of tape recorders and synthesizers. The Indian subcontinent has slowly adapted to these developments, for example, in film music, due to its sluggish cultural mobility. Even then, the synthesizer made its way, mainly because subcontinental elites, like the Sarabhai family, stood for a modernist change.

This book documents the travels of the synthesizer in detail and helps the readers to comprehend how the machine was able to make a short but revolutionary movement, enabling the disentanglement of sound from the cultural roots of traditional instrumentation. Historically, no one could touch a sarod or a sitar until the guru had taught a student how to play them—the subcontinent had a hierarchical and often feudal approach to music-making. The synthesizer became a sonic instrument that appeared without these traditional clutches. The people who gathered around it and considered it a laboratory object, a situation for pure experimentation, saw the instrument as accessible without much cultural conditioning. This sense of democratic freedom to experiment was unique—as we hear from some of the contributors to this book. Many of the NID composers stopped making music, but the short period of sheer experimentation and freedom to research enriched their worldviews and opened their pathways. The synthesizer legitimized and validated the right to experiment and innovate. This experimental spirit and the emergent ideas followed the sounds to reach the vibrant areas of cultural life like inaudible ripples, from film music to television, popular music to radio, and everyday practices. Although the arrival of the synthesizer might have seemed disjunct, the ramifications were complexly enmeshed with the subcontinent's desire to self-determine.

The Moog Synthesiser: Electronic Music and a Design Institute in India
Shilpa Das

After India became an independent nation in 1947, the country's visionaries, planners and leaders were faced with the monumental task of nation building. Several institutions of science, technology, arts and media were established across the epoque-defining 1950s that embodied India's cultural heritage with the new mantra of self-determination. They strove to achieve a fine balance between evolving a modern Indian consciousness whilst concurrently reaffirming India's age old cultural identity. As industrialisation became the new republic's prime concern to complement the Nehruvian vision of a modern forward-looking Indian state, a vanguard of new technical and managerial professionals had to be developed to support this programme for national growth, and it was inevitable that sooner or later, modern design would become a necessity. After the Second World War, the Western world had witnessed an unprecedented explosion of design that was reminiscent of a new Industrial Revolution. Now, having overthrown the yoke of centuries of British colonial oppression, a euphoric India radiating a new-found optimism and belief in its own potential became "the most vibrant site for the "modern project", where the East-West relationship was constantly redefined and the modernizing experience was key in forming the nation's identity."[1]

← Akhil Succena assessing slides at the NID circa 1970.

It was under these circumstances that in 1957, the Indian government requested the Ford Foundation to invite the celebrated American designers Charles and Ray Eames to visit India. On April 7, 1958, based on the sum total of their experiences across the country, the duo presented the Indian Government with an evocative piece of literature called the *India Report* which delineated an appropriate design perspective for the country drawing upon the "talismanic metaphor"[2] of the humble Indian lota and exhorted the founding of a design institute of national importance to shape the new industrial India. Its presentation marked the beginning of design as a profession in India.[3] In 1960, the Ford Foundation commissioned Ernst Scheidegger from Switzerland and Vilhelm Wohlert from Denmark as consultants to devise plans to set up the proposed design institute. The report they submitted emphasised that education and training must become the cornerstones of the institute, and the workshop was to be adopted as the node of design education.[4]

The city of Ahmedabad, already an important commercial centre, had become the capital of the newly formed state of Gujarat with its strong Gandhian legacy and the progressive outlook and innovative spirit of its industrialists and mill owners, who understood the importance of keeping in step with the time in order to compete in a global market. Ahmedabad represented a new set of values, and claimed an important position in the nation-building programme, quickly becoming an epicentre of an institution building exercise with experiments in education at its core.

The Sarabhais were one such influential business family with an international reputation and connections. The respected and philanthropic Ambalal Sarabhai, a strong supporter of Mahatma Gandhi and the founder of Calico Mills (one of Ahmedabad's oldest textile mills), contributed significantly to the fields of commerce, education, science, arts, and architecture. Their home hosted the leading lights of the time— from leaders of India's struggle for independence such as Mahatma Gandhi, Jawaharlal Nehru, Mohammad Ali Jinnah to several luminaries from the fields of art, music, architecture, literature, education and design, including Nobel Laureates Rabindranath Tagore and Sir C.V. Raman, Le Corbusier, Louis Kahn, Alexander Calder, Isamu Noguchi, Buckminster Fuller, Frei Otto, John Cage, Richard Neutra, Henri Cartier-Bresson, Maxwell Fry, Merce Cunningham, Roy Lichtenstein, Stella Kramrisch, Robert Rauschenberg, E.M. Forster and Maria Montessori, amongst a host of others.[5]

The National Industrial Design Institute (later called the National Institute of Design or NID) was set up in this context in 1961 to foster an indigenous design movement in the modern sense of the word and a programme to shape this new profession. Its establishment resulted from the amalgam of several global and local forces, that gradually gained momentum and converged at that precise historical time: the legacy of the former schools of arts and crafts, inroads made by the Modern Movement in India, the onset of industrialisation in India, expanding international efforts to promote design in the industrial sector, the heritage of traditional Indian craft and design, the Industrial Policy Resolution of 1953, a fortuitous meeting of Pupul Jayakar and Charles Eames at MoMA in New York, financial support extended by the Ford Foundation, the *India Report*, the formation of the new state of Gujarat in 1960 and emergence of Ahmedabad as its capital city, and last but not the least, the radical vision and untiring efforts of the NID's founding parents, Gautam and Gira Sarabhai, the first a mathematician and the second, an architect who had trained with Frank Lloyd Wright.

Gautam Sarabhai avoided the conventional methods of education, which instructed through a sequential exploration of theory and practice whilst giving primacy to theory, and instead explored alternative approaches which incorporated radical education models and pedagogies. He followed the Bauhaus dictum *"learning by doing"* that promoted a simultaneous learning of theory and practice and rephrased it as *"learning to know and learning to do."*[6] In 1963, Jesse Reichek, Professor of Design at the University of California, who was invited to Ahmedabad to contribute towards the concept-building of the institute, urged on practice and production processes as tools for design education. He also insisted that guest designers from India and overseas should be invited to the institute for short stays to bring 'real life experience" to the institute's doorstep and provide practical training under their guidance to the regular staff and students, thus contributing to a widening of their global understanding and experience. Workshops and studios were to be established in keeping with Gautam Sarabhai's vision and Reichek's report.[7]

NID's sound studio was set up between 1964 and 1968 through funds given by Ford Foundation and with the help of R. Tolat who had overseen Gandhi's public address system in Ahmedabad. The audio equipment was loaned by Gira Sarabhai and comprised a Berlant 7" spool tape recorder, a Shure microphone, and Ahuja amplifiers, used

Hasu Qureshi, Akhil Succena, Amritlal Kalal (standing) and S.C Sharma
in the sound studio circa 1970.

for recording and reproduction between 1964 and 1966. NID also acquired a Thorens turntable, AKG microphones, Ampex ¼" magnetic tape recorders, and Tannoy speakers to start a basic recording studio. Previously Ampex recorders had only been used at All India Radio and cartridges of the Thorens turntables, manufactured in the US, were procured with great difficulty. Electronic equipment was also not easily available in Ahmedabad and had to bought from Lamington Road in Bombay. Two Nagra ¼" recorders were imported for outdoor recording. Along with Nagra recorders, Zeinhauser microphones were also used.[8] The driving force behind these acquisitions was that Gautam and Gira Sarabhai were always conscious to learn about and acquire state-of-the-art audio-visual equipment and spared no expense in creating infrastructural space or acquisitioning hardware for the young institute in order to bring contemporary technology directly to the NID. This was also because the institute's earliest projects were large-scale exhibitions in which the soundscape played a pivotal role. I.S. Mathur, a graduate in Film Technology from the Institute of Film Technology, Madras and one of NID's foremost students in Visual Communication was in charge of the equipment. He subsequently started the former Film and Sound department at the NID but the sound studio was very much its progenitor.[9]

At that point in the nascent institute, a structured curriculum was absent, and instead a fluid approach was adopted that proved to be appropriate for introducing diverse themes, fresh disciplines and new sensibilities to the students. Gira put I.S. Mathur in touch with her sister Gita Sarabhai (also known as Geeta Mayor), a musicologist, renowned patron of music and a highly respected musician who was one of the first female pakhavaj (a percussion instrument) players in India. It was Gita who helped the respected American avant garde composer of the twentieth century, John Cage, understand the technicalities and aesthetics of Indian classical music. She had met Cage in 1946 in the US when she stayed there for several months learning about Western music, concerned as she was about the influence of Western musical modernity on Indian classical music traditions. She and Cage agreed upon a mutual education exchange: she would teach Cage the nuances of Indian music and he would teach her the essentials of contemporary Western music.

This is the backdrop to the establishment of the innovative and experimental electronic sound studio at that National Institute of Design that functioned between 1969 and 1972 with funds from the Ford Foundation. The New York based pianist, composer, music theorist and electronic musician David Tudor who had famously collaborated with John Cage, initiated and established the studio when he travelled to India in autumn 1969. Tudor was invited by Gita Sarabhai (on behalf of Gautam and Gira Sarabhai), and oversaw the shipping of a brand new Moog modular synthesiser in wooden crates from New York prior to his departure. He stayed in Ahmedabad for three months, during which he installed not only the Moog but also a series of tape machines to create a distinctive electronic music studio. He conducted a workshop on live electronic music with the Moog for students and staff from NID. This experiment with sound caught the attention of eminent scientist and brother of the Sarabhai siblings, Vikram Sarabhai, who attended the sessions too.[10]

One evening in 1969, a programme called *Soundscape*, a light and sound display, was organised across the campus at NID at Gita Sarabhai's behest and about 20,000 people from the city came for the event. Students and staff at NID excitedly experimented with this new and strange seeming instrument playfully creating futuristic and "abstract" sounds in the form of electronic music for the very first time. This was also the first time that electronic music made inroads into the country. The Moog occupied 20 x 15ft of prime space in an acoustically fitted room, along with a collection of amplifiers and speakers.[11] The Visual Communication department at the time had only four students and they had a 12-week sound course. The emphasis was placed on sound as a primary medium and not just as a secondary aspect of film.

One of those four students was Dhun Karkaria who played on the Moog whenever he had free time. I visited him at his studio in 2012, and Karkaria showed me the Moog he had bought from the NID in the 1980s which he said was in mint condition save one key. He said, "We were introduced to that great piece of equipment where you generate music, not from an analogue source such as a musical instrument or a voice but at a wave form level...sine wave, square wave, triangular wave and others. It also possessed a monosyllabic keyboard. You cannot play chords on it but only one key at a time, more or less like you play the harmonium. There is an accentuating wire and it would create different frequencies if you placed a finger on the wire. If one hand played the keyboard, another was on the accentuating wire. I became very fond of that piece of equipment; whenever I had spare time, I would play it. Years later, the equipment had become outdated, was lying unused, and was being auctioned. I bid for it and got it. It was the only piece to arrive in India."[12] Another student of the time who did many free-spirited experimentations with the Moog to explore its possibilities in the sound studio after his classes was Dadi Pudumjee (now one of India's renowned puppeteers). The use of the Moog by students, judiciously limited and controlled, continued after Tudor left until about 1973.

I.S. Mathur reminisced about how Tudor taught them electronic music on the Moog by "patching the cords." One of Mathur's own compositions on the Moog was titled "Moogsical Forms"[13] clearly inspired by the idiosyncrasies of the instrument. He also produced some

rare recordings of renowned artists such as Vilayat Khan and Rasoolan
Bai in the initial years, alongside sound recordings on a Nagra 3 recorder
for the India Pavilion at the 1967 Montreal Expo, in which he worked
with Dashrath Patel and Tudor to create an audioscape, conceived as an
environment using electronic sounds.

In 1968, S.C. Sharma, an audiographer from the Film and Television
Institute (FTII) Pune joined the studio, and subsequently managed
most of the sound recordings. Sharma went on to produce some unique
minimal proto-techno sonic explorations at the NID. Akhil Succena,
a young sound engineering graduate also from the FTII assisted the
sound studio in 1973 and stayed with the institute until 2010. He recalls
that Sharma had a magical personality and the heart of a poet. He had
a big fan following both within NID and outside, and hosted elaborate
meals at his home.[14] I.S. Mathur once said of him that he wrote beautiful
poetry in Hindi, had a magical voice and delighted in presenting readings
to his colleagues. He explained that Sharma was a workaholic, ready to
take on anything, known to work long hours at the studio and deliver work
of a high quality.[15] Reportedly, he had a mercurial temperament, it was
always "his way or the highway", and sparks flew daily between Mathur
(who could be irascible himself) and Sharma. Nonetheless, Mathur
commented that Akhil Succena was "extraordinary material for a team,
would give his opinion on work related matters but not confront and also
readily internalised design, design thinking and design education, big
requisites in a design institute. Your role in a design institute including
with respect to sound is communication after all."[16]

In 2017, British artist and musician Paul Purgas discovered
a collection of reel-to-reel tapes from the electronic music studio archive
that chronicled three years of radical sonic experiments across almost
30 hours of audio recordings, including S.C. Sharma's "Dance Music"
and Jinraj Joshipura's "Space Liner 2001" compositions. Purgas also
discovered two recordings produced by Gita Sarabhai which he explains
"seek to explicitly map musicality onto the Moog itself."[17] Succena says
"since the Moog was an electronic instrument it was rather experimental
for its time, did not have its own set scale, it lent itself to improvisation
in terms of scale but it was hard to categorise the output as music. It
was more of an expression. People would explore what they could do
with it. Those with a musical mind would attempt to play it as a musical
instrument and those who did not would experiment with it. They'd say,

for instance, this is like "a bird chirping" or this is like "the sound of rain". So they'd create the sounds and then name them based on what they got. After a point, it got unruly and so we had to regulate the time that students like Dhun could come and play on it."[18]

Vispi Siganporia, a well-known musician and drummer in Ahmedabad who started the rock bands Black Beats and Purple Flower, visited the NID as a young man to meet his cousin, Dhun, and play on the Moog. He says that the Moog modular system at the NID "required a lot of patching which was not easy to do," and to his great disappointment was used "more for creating patterns on it, and not so much for sound." Very soon, in the early 1970s, several Minimoogs came to be used in India in jazz concerts including the Jazz-Yatra held in Bombay's Rang Bhavan that Vispi and Dhun would drive their motorcycles over 300 miles from Ahmedabad to attend.

The eminent Hindustani classical vocalist and composer, Atul Desai also frequented NID's sound studio and attended David Tudor's classes. Desai's wife, Sandhya Desai, a distinguished Kathak dancer, recalls that Desai lectured at the NID once a month on sound and music, and became good friends with I.S. Mathur and S.C. Sharma.[19] Besides contributing music to contemporary dance choreography and especially to the Kadamb School of Dance (Kathak) in Ahmedabad, run by notable danseuse Kumudini Lakhia, Atul Desai was also a highly respected artistic contributor to All India Radio from where his programmes were broadcast regularly. Desai met "the very jovial, very informal and very simple" Tudor over cups of coffee at Manorama Sarabhai's home. He was excited by the avant-garde composer's experimental oeuvre and learnt electronic music from Tudor not only when he conducted the workshops at the NID, but also a few years later, at John Cage's studio in the US when he travelled with Kumudini Lakhia's dance troupe on a tour to New York for a month and a half. Sandhya Desai described Tudor as "a dynamic person with an exceptional spark and a patient teacher." Atul Desai was interested in "naad" or pure sounds such as that of the Om and readily took to the Moog to explore these concepts. He had long discussions with Tudor, and created a number of sound experiments on it including those of a barking dog as well as cosmic sounds. All this led Desai to set up his own electronic sound studio, *Dhvani*, in his home in Ahmedabad. Sharma, whom Sandhya describes as "a simple and creative person; a part of our lives like a family member" played a pivotal role in

David Tudor with S.C. Sharma, in Ahmedabad 1969.

helping Desai set up his studio, working night and day at their home. Desai and he would have animated discussions all night making plans for the studio, jamming, and Sharma even wrote the script in Hindi and English and poetic couplets for a dance play named "Karna" that Kumudini Lakhia's troupe including Sandhya performed in Chicago. For the Indian Pavilion at the 1970 Expo in Osaka, Tudor recommended Atul Desai's name and the NID invited him to represent the Institute. Vikram Sarabhai was in charge of the Indian Pavilion and asked Desai to create an ambience of sounds through an Indian soundscape—a sound track of electronic sounds created on the Moog that would play on a loop.

Once Tudor left Ahmedabad, the studio was used by a number of Indian composers from the city and other places, recalls Succena.[20] By then, a United Nations Development Programme grant had enabled the purchase of two bulky Ampex 350 deck recorders, and two small Ampex 2000 portable recorders that could be taken outside to locations for recording as well as other Foley equipment. All the hardware was housed in a beautifully designed studio which was a lively space with sound recordings going on all the time. This ignited the curiosity of other staff especially those from the Industrial Design department at the NID to whom the studio looked like a "NASA type control room" and who questioned the relevance of the equipment in a design institute. Succena adds that the studio was an integral part of documentary films made by NID, and from 1972 onwards, it also regularly recorded sound for radio plays and radio advertisements (spots or jingles). Those days the only other sound studio in the city was at All India Radio, the local radio station, and their policy did not allow for public use.

The NID received several requests from advertisers to be allowed to record at its studio as they had to travel all the way to Bombay for recordings. Sharma and Succena interceded with the management and got permission to do the recordings after official hours. The musicians, who held regular jobs elsewhere, would pour into the studio around 8pm and the recordings would go on all night until the early hours of the morning. As news spread that NID had a sound recording studio, Gujarati film producers approached NID to do recordings for feature films. This complemented the skills learnt through many of NID's early international and national exhibition projects that were sponsored by various ministries that required soundtracks to be created with a diorama to enhance the viewers' sense of the exhibition space. Sometimes, they needed soundtracks with a narration, such as folktales read by radio announcer Ameen Sayani produced for the *Festival of India* exhibition in London. Succena says that both he and Sharma enjoyed themselves thoroughly in that "heady time".

From the chronology of the tapes it appears that Sharma did the very last recording with the Moog in 1972. That was to be amongst its last journeys. As around this time the Institute's experimental pedagogical programme and the Moog itself were heavily criticized by the Indian government bureaucrats as the proverbial white elephant, an extravagant, impetuous and indulgent acquisition by the Sarabhais with no direct application or relevance to design education. The Sarabhais resigned and left the National Institute of Design in 1973 and it heralded the end of an era.

Notes

1   Rahul Mehrotra. "Architecture and Indian Identity", in *Architecture in India since 1990* (Mumbai: Pictor Publishing, 2011) 30.

2   Eames Demetrios. *An Eames Primer.* London: Thames and Hudson, 2001.

3   Charles Eames and Ray Eames. *The India Report.* Los Angeles, April 1958.

4   Ernst Scheidegger and Vilhelm Wohlert. *Proposal for an Institute of Design, Training, Service and Research.* New Delhi, June 1960.

5   Aparna Basu. *As Times Change: The Story of an Ahmedabad Business Family, The Sarabhais, 1823–1975.* Ahmedabad: Sarabhai Foundation, 2018.

6   Shilpa Das (ed.), *50 Years of the National Institute of Design: 1961–2011.* Ahmedabad: NID, 2013.

7   Jesse Reichek. *Report to the Governing Council.* Ahmedabad: 1963.

8   I.S. Mathur, email to Shilpa Das, 2012. Validated by Akhil Succena in an online interview with Shilpa Das on February 25, 2022.

9   I.S. Mathur, conversation with Shilpa Das, 2011.

10   Sandhya Desai in an online interview with Shilpa Das, February 10, 2022.

11   Akhil Succena in an online interview with Shilpa Das on February 25, 2022.

12   Dhun Karkaria, conversation with the author, August 2012.

13   I.S. Mathur, conversation with Shilpa Das, 2011.

14   Akhil Succena in an online interview with Shilpa Das on February 25, 2022.

15   I.S. Mathur, conversation with Shilpa Das, 2011.

16   I.S. Mathur, conversation with Shilpa Das, 2011.

17   Paul Purgas in an interview with Frances Morgan, "Electronic India: 1969–73 Revisited." May 17, 2020. https://www.thewire.co.uk/in-writing/interviews/electronic-india-moog-interview-paul-purgas.

18   Akhil Succena in an online interview with Shilpa Das on February 25, 2022.

19   Sandhya Desai in an online interview with Shilpa Das, February 10, 2022.

On Karma: Incidents and Influences in India and Far Beyond
You Nakai

1

Sometime in the mid-1940s, a young musician living in Ahmedabad, India, became "concerned about the influence Western music was having on traditional Indian music."[1] She happened to be one of the eight siblings of the Sarabhai family, who had amassed a great fortune in the local textile industry which originally burgeoned under British rule, and then used that fortune to support Mahatma Gandhi to drive the same rulers out. And the patriarch Ambalal, who took great pride in defending the tradition of his country against external influences, happened to share his daughter's concern and had the money to support her cause. So in 1946, just a year before Gandhi accomplished his cause of making India independent, the twenty-four-year-old Gita Sarabhai "decided to study Western music for six months" in New York, and "then return to India to do what she could to preserve the Indian traditions."[2] It was a peculiar idea that resembled the principle of vaccination: she was to deliberately expose herself to the source of influence in order to become immune to it—or, at least that was the plan.

   In fact, what Gita did when she arrived in New York was not to study diligently at Juilliard as she initially intended, but to incidentally befriend a thirty-four-year-old composer who offered to teach her Western music and counterpoint for free in exchange for her teaching him about Indian music. She agreed and they were "almost every day together."[3] And then, she headed home.[4]

This story is well-known because the American composer included it in the collection of short stories he amassed from his life and readings which he later published and performed under the title of *Indeterminacy.*[5] His name was John Cage, and the influence of Gita's teaching on his music and philosophy has been widely discussed.[6] In particular, as Cage recalled during a lecture-performance in October 1954, the musician who came halfway across the planet to learn how to deal with the influence of Western music had some important things to say about a different kind of influence:

> Years ago I asked myself
> "Why do I write music?"
> An Indian musician told me the
> traditional answer in India was
> "To sober the mind and thus make
> it susceptible to divine influences."[7]

This traditional answer would become one of the proverbs that the composer incited over and over again throughout the years to describe the purpose of his otherwise purposeless music.[8] But the story doesn't end there, for Cage was obviously not the only susceptible one in this incidental exchange.

2

In early September 1958, Cage appeared at the International Summer Courses for New Music in Darmstadt, Germany, giving a joint presentation on the topic of *Indeterminacy*, which went on to exert great influence on European avant-garde music that many people would soon become concerned about. He was accompanied by the pianist and multi-instrumentalist David Tudor, who provided musical examples of what Cage talked about. The duo subsequently embarked on a tour across Europe, traveling and performing through Cologne, Stockholm, Copenhagen, Warsaw, Brussels, and Düsseldorf, arriving in London on October 16. Four days later, Tudor wrote home to his then-partner M.C. Richards: "we are staying at Manorama Sarabhai's flat & in a few minutes will eat an Indian lunch."⁹ Through Cage's connection to Gita, he had befriended another member of the Sarabhai family: Manorama Sarabhai, the wife of Gita's brother Suhrid who happened to be living in England at the time, far away from her home in Ahmedabad, the famous Villa Sarabhai she had commissioned Le Corbusier to build seven years earlier. A week later, Tudor sent a follow-up letter to Richards from Hamburg reflecting warmly on his encounter: "it was very pleasant to be in England even tho our engagements didn't amount to much—we spent many hours with our friend Priaulx Rainier & with Manorama Sarabhai, who is a wonderful woman. She is going to send me things from India."¹⁰

By "things," Tudor most certainly meant something edible, as their friendship would increasingly be anchored in a shared love of cooking. As Asha Sarabhai, the wife of Manorama's son Suhrid Jr., looked back much later in 2015: "The whole food thing was a very important connection because my mother-in-law was passionate about food and knew everything about Indian food. So there was a big exchange there in terms of culinary, but she also was an incredibly cordial and generous and very powerful kind of woman. [...] she and David Tudor were good friends."¹¹

Three years after their first encounter, Tudor again passed through London, this time on his own. He stayed with Manorama, reporting again to Richards on November 28, 1961: "Have been with Mani in London for a few days—she gets lovelier every year."¹² And after Manorama returned to India the following summer, it was Tudor alone who accepted their friend's ardent invitation and made a detour after his tour in Japan with Cage, to stop by Ahmedabad and spend time with her family for two weeks in November 1962. Sixteen years after Gita's fortuitous foray into the experimental music of New York, the experimental music of New York had reached back to Ahmedabad in the form of David Tudor.

3

By this time, however, Tudor may have developed another special interest in India besides the excellent food. On August 10, 1965, Manorama wrote a letter asking Tudor to remind her what it was that he was looking for during his first visit: "When you were here two years back you wanted a book on anthropology or something (I do not remember). If you write to me the name, I shall try + locate it for you. You said that it is only possible (if at all) to find it in India."[13] The book Tudor had in mind was most probably not on anthropology but on anthroposophy, the occult philosophy initiated by Rudolf Steiner in the early twentieth century of which Tudor was an avid yet idiosyncratic follower. The multi-instrumentalist had become a member of the Anthroposophical Society in July 1957 when he abruptly cancelled his scheduled appearance at the International Summer Courses for New Music in Darmstadt and instead spent his days going to the Anthroposophy Summer School. On October 25, 1962, two weeks before his first visit to Ahmedabad, Tudor sent a word of advice to M.C. Richards who had begun reading Steiner under his influence: "about joining the AS, Eleanor Minne told me when I inquired about joining, that all my karmic relationships would be accelerated—& this I have found true most astoundingly, & continues to be so & will continue—& one is thus called upon to make decisions about one's life (whether one does so or not) that would otherwise not have occurred (& one is aware of that too). I have no better advice than that."[14]

The connection between anthroposophy and Ahmedabad was yet another story of incidental cultural exchange. Anthroposophy had begun in 1912 as an offshoot of the Theosophical Society, whose German section had been led by Steiner for ten years by then. The issue that prompted the Austrian esotericist and self-claimed clairvoyant to go his own way revolved around India of all places. In February 1879, Helena Blavatsky, who had founded the Theosophical Society just four years before in New York, suddenly relocated to Bombay after the movement had lost its initial momentum in the West. Taking as her model the spiritualist novels penned by Lord Edward George Bulwer-Lytton who also happened to be the Secretary of State for the Colonies of the United Kingdom, Blavatsky had first claimed to have personally encountered occult Masters in Egypt before changing the setting of her story to Tibet—which conveniently made India the place to be. During her time there, she proceeded to mix elements of Hinduism and Buddhism into her teachings, and Theosophy, in turn, spread like fire throughout

→ Fig 01

HEAD OFFICE: 24 ST. MARY AXE
LONDON. E. C. 3

SARABHAI AGENCIES

BRANCH OF

BAKUBHAI & AMBALAL, LTD.

(INCORPORATED IN GREAT BRITAIN)

30 ROCKEFELLER PLAZA

NEW YORK, N. Y. 10020

TELEPHONE: PLAZA 7-8450-1-2
CABLES: SARAVEPAR-NEW YORK

March 15th, 1968

Ref:12409

Mr. David Tudor
Gat Hill Road
Stony Point, New York 10980

Dear Mr. Tudor:

In reference to our telephone conversation, I have enclosed herewith the detailed specifications with photographs of the Synket Equipment. Miss Gira Sarabhai would like to have your advice and opinion on the same as this equipment is offered to her for National Design Institute, with which she is actively associated. She would very much appreciate to know from you if you have any other equipment to recommend. I now look forward for your reply on your return from your trip.

I take the opportunity to thank you for your assistance and cooperation.

With best regards,

Yours sincerely,

A. R. Mehta

EXTENDED VOICES

NEW PIECES FOR CHORUS AND FOR VOICES ALTERED
ELECTRONICALLY BY SOUND SYNTHESIZERS AND VOCODER
THE BRANDEIS UNIVERSITY CHAMBER CHORUS
ALVIN LUCIER, DIRECTOR

ROBERT ASHLEY: SHE WAS A VISITOR
JOHN CAGE: SOLOS FOR VOICE 2
[ELECTRONIC REALIZATION BY GORDON MUMMA AND DAVID TUDOR]
MORTON FELDMAN: CHORUS AND INSTRUMENTS II
CHRISTIAN WOLFF IN CAMBRIDGE
TOSHI ICHYANAGI: EXTENDED VOICES
[FOR VOICES WITH MOOG SYNTHESIZER AND
BUCHLA ASSOCIATES ELECTRONIC MODULAR SYSTEM]
ALVIN LUCIER: NORTH AMERICAN TIME CAPSULE 1967
[FOR VOICES AND SYLVANIA ELECTRONIC SYSTEMS VOCODER]
PAULINE OLIVEROS: SOUND PATTERNS

Fig 02

various religious movements in the country.[15] In particular, Blavatsky's praise of Indian religion and criticism of British imperialism made her popular among the local elites before she left for England in 1884 and succumbed to influenza seven years later at the age of 59.

The consequence of her fortuitous foray into the subcontinent lived on, however, and Annie Besant, who succeeded Blavatsky as the president of the Theosophical Society, became convinced that Jiddu Krishnamurti, a South Indian boy she had met at the Indian headquarters in Madras, was the World Teacher and reincarnation of Christ. All this was too much to take for Steiner who was more inclined towards Christian mysticism and was concerned about the influence Eastern religion was having on traditional European spiritualism.[16] So they parted ways—though one side effect of this history was preserved in the form of rare book on anthroposophy Tudor was looking for on his first trip to Ahmedabad, which he seemed to believe he could only find there.

4

Thus, a multi-layered network of influences had emanated in and out of India for quite some time to stage Tudor's visit. As it happens, one of the recurrent topics in Steiner's teachings was none other than "influence," the occult flowing of essence from one entity to another that this teacher of esotericism traced all the way back to the ancient belief in the powers of stars and planets (most notably theorized by the Neo-Platonists in the third century and revived later in Renaissance astrology).[17] According to this long-lasting view, ethereal fluids emanating from celestial bodies triggered all sorts of effects on earth without themselves being sensed, one among which was the sudden outbreak of malady known as influenza, and another was the modification of incidental turn of events which some call fortuitous.

This was a teaching Tudor took much to heart and applied specifically when describing the relationship between electronic instruments which was replete with indeterminacy: "A lot of components I made myself, most of them processing components somewhat like you would for a synthesiser. But with a synthesiser you match up each component with the next one, so that each input can handle the previous output. I found out that if the components don't match, then one component is able to *influence* the next, so that signals are created at many points within the circuit."[18] The same word also applied to the relationship between himself and his instruments that, as he once described, "you could only hope to *influence.*"[19] And to the question of why he delved more and more into that kind of instrument, Tudor had revealed, at least on one occasion, the particular kind of influence that drove him: "alcohol goes very well with electronic music; it's not so good with piano playing!"[20]

5

On March 15, 1968, A.R. Mehta from the New York branch of Sarabhai Agencies sent a letter to Tudor which relayed a message from Ahmedabad [FIG 01]:

> In reference to our telephone conversation, I have enclosed herewith the detailed specifications with photographs of the Synket Equipment. Miss Gira Sarabhai would like to have your advice and opinion on the same as this equipment is offered to her for National Design Institute, with which she is actively associated. She would very much appreciate to know from you if you have any other equipment to recommend.[21]

Gira, the younger sister of Gita and Manorama, had worked together with their brother Gautam in setting up the National Institute of Design in their hometown back in 1961. Now a plan had emerged to establish the country's first electronic music studio inside the same institute, and Gira was asking their family friend who, since around the time he met Manorama, had been delving deep into the world of electronic music and its occult influences.

The "Synket Equipment" mentioned in the letter was a synthesizer that the Italian sound engineer Paul Ketoff had built in 1963. Nicely equipped with a square wave generator, frequency dividers, filters, and modulators controlled with three small keyboards, it had gained some following: the American composer John Eaton used it a lot, as well as many Spaghetti Western movies. But this synthesizer was not conceived as a commercial product, and the dozen or so models Ketoff made were all custom-made one-off instruments. So, it wouldn't be surprising if Tudor had advised Gira to think of different equipment instead. In fact, the letter itself documents the trace of another instrument that might have been on Tudor's mind as he communicated with the Sarabhai Agencies, for the name of one synthesizer module that does not belong to the Synket is scribbled down in the margin: "912 envelope follower"—a unit to produce a control voltage proportional to the envelope of the input signal (allowing one sound to influence another), designed by Robert Moog.[22]

                                    → Fig 03

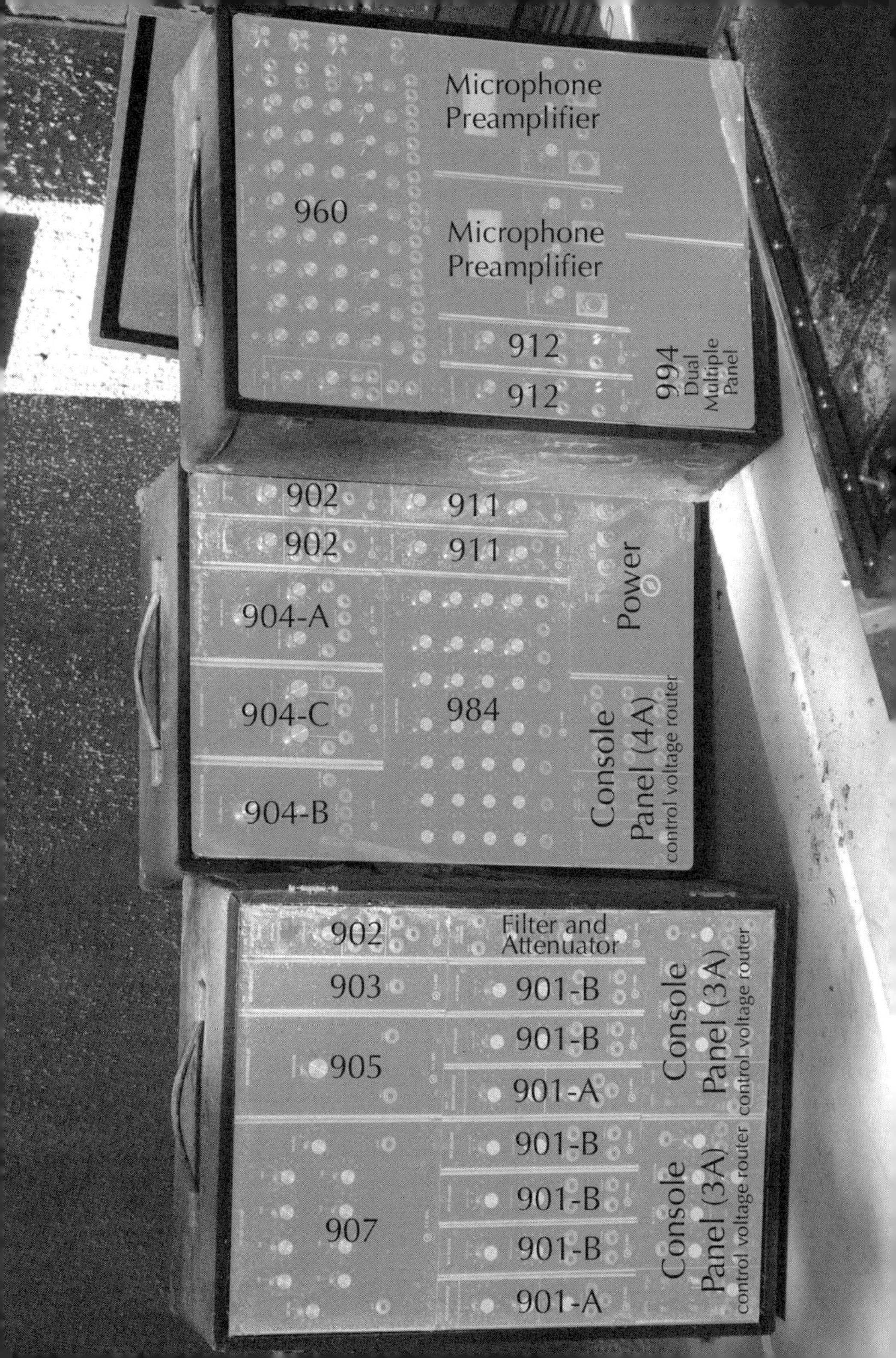

Microphone
Preamplifier

960

Microphone
Preamplifier

912

912

994
Dual
Multiple
Panel

902   911
902   911

904-A

904-C   984

904-B

Power

Console
Panel (4A)
control voltage router

902   Filter and
       Attenuator
903   901-B
       901-B
905   901-A
       901-B
       901-B
907   901-B
       901-A

Console
Panel (3A)
control voltage router

Console
Panel (3A)
control voltage router

Tudor was no stranger to either Moog or his instruments. In July 1965, Moog provided twelve capacitance-sensitive antennae for *Variations V,* a multi-media collaboration between Cage and Merce Cunningham, in which the proximity of dancers on stage to the 5-foot-high metallic poles triggered sounds performed by Tudor and Cage. Later that year, Tudor called Moog up to discuss the construction of a touch-sensitive control device. But Tudor did not hide the fact that he hated the so-called synthesizers that made Moog famous. His complaint was mostly against the inflexibility caused by standardization, which resulted in predictability—a loss of fortuity. As he explained in September 1984: "I hated the way those machines were so predictable; and it's very difficult to make them sound, you know, different than they're supposed to."[23]

But despite this dislike, it is quite possible that Tudor suggested the Moog synthesizer in his reply to Gira. This was March 1968, and he had been fiddling around with such commercial electronic instruments for about a year, finding a way to make them sound different than they're supposed to. For seven weeks since December of the previous year, Tudor was a guest lecturer at Mills Tape Music Center in Oakland, California, where he had enjoyed wrestling with the Buchla synthesizer that was installed there. Anthony Gnazzo, who worked at Mills at the time, recalled Tudor's distinct approach to the instrument: "David's favorite patch on the Buchla which he used to demonstrate to his students, was one where he would feed the output of a device through one of the mixers back into the input, i.e. howling feedback. I don't recall that he ever tried any other patch."[24]

Several months before, Tudor had also made a recording of Cage's *Solo for Voice No. 2* to be included in the *Extended Voices* LP produced by David Behrman. Gordon Mumma, who collaborated with Tudor on this realization, recently remembered what they did: "For that we used —e.g. Subverted—the possibilities of both Moog and Buchla synthesizers—then being in their relatively early development."[25] Later, he added a correction: "more subvert the Moog things, not the Buchla things."[26] [FIG 02] And so, quite fortuitously, by the time the inquiry came from Ahmedabad, Tudor had developed some hands-on knowledge on the kinds of commercial instruments being considered.

→ Fig 04

David Tudor
Willow Grove Rd.
Stony Point, N.Y. 10980

Equipment list for Seminar in Electronic Music, in
Ahmedabad, India, October through December, 1969

1 Case, 28" x 14" x 8"

Contents:	Value
1 Bag of miscellaneous sound cables & adapters	85.00
2 Lafayette mixers, PA-292	10.00
5 Phase shifters, custom built	150.00
2 Tone controls (with power units), custom built	50.00
1 Substitution box, custom built	20.00
2 AA-100 amplifiers, custom built	20.00
1 Signal adder, custom built	10.00
1 Olson RA 637 mixer-preamp	35.00
1 Lafayette preamp, custom built	10.00
2 Olson phono preamps, AM-287	12.00
1 Sony wireless microphone, CRT-30 (made in Japan)	21.00
1 Bias-box, custom built	5.00
1 Frequency divider, custom built	15.00
2 Pulse generators, custom built	50.00
1 Switching box, custom built	10.00
1 Nombrex audio generator (made in U.K.)	45.00
1 Cybersonics output splitter	80.00
2 Dual mike preamps, custom built	50.00
1 Sound stirrer, custom built	100.00
2 Waveform generators, custom built	20.00
2 Ring modulators, custom built	25.00
1 Teley headset	10.00
1 Harmonic generator, custom built	5.00
Total —	838.00

6

Thus, the Moog synthesizer was chosen as the primary instrument to be installed at the National Institute of Design, and Tudor was invited to offer his expertise to get the job done.[27] As early as March 1, 1969, Manorama wrote excitedly to her friend: "I have heard from Gira that you may be coming to the Design Institute some time this year. May I ask you to be my guest for the duration that you will be in India. It would be such a wonderful thing."[28] She had to wait another seven months, during which time Tudor kept in contact with the Sarabhai Agencies to select other equipment to populate the new studio.[29]

Tudor travelled to India probably in the second week of October, along with a whole set of Moog synthesizer modules which were shipped from the Moog factory in Trumansburg, New York. He kept a series of dated schematics that Moog had sent him for this task—twenty-one modules, to be exact.[30] The modules corresponding to the schematics can all be identified in the extant photograph of the NID Moog, revealing the specific configuration of the instrument Tudor installed in Ahmedabad.[31] [FIG 03]

But the Moog synthesizer was not the only instrument that travelled halfway across the planet with Tudor. Aside from setting up the studio, he had been asked to conduct a seminar on electronic music. So, Tudor brought along his own instruments whose identity is revealed by a list of equipment he prepared for custom declaration. [FIG 04, 05] These are all instruments that he was using in his performances at the time, a mixed bag of custom-build devices and commercial products, which, unlike synthesizer modules, did not match with one another for the sake of influence.[32]

According to the reminiscence of Jinraj Joshipura who participated in Tudor's workshop, NID gave out fliers in advance asking people to come and join the seminar led by "the director of the Institute of Experiments in Art and Technology," who, along with John Cage, had "taught the Beatles electronic music synthesizer just two months before coming to Ahmedabad."[33] As a result of this grand publicity, nine people showed up for the workshop, from which three dropped out eventually. None of the remaining six members, Joshipura recalls, were NID students, including himself who was a student in a nearby school of architecture, several faculty members of NID (I.S. Mathur and S.C. Sharma), and

1 CASE , 24" x 14" x 7"

CONTENTS:	VALUE
1 EDITALL SPLICING BLOCK	6.50
1 LAFAYETTE CR SUBSTITUTION BOX	5.00
1 SINCLAIR STEREO 25 PREAMP (MADE IN U.K.)	25.00
2 SINCLAIR MICRO FM RECEIVERS (MADE IN U.K.)	36.00
1 CLARICON MULTITESTER	14.00
1 UNGAR SOLDERING PEN	8.00
1 VACUVISE	6.00
BOXES CONTAINING SPARE ELECTRONIC PARTS & HARDWARE	100.00
BAGS CONTAINING TOOLS, CLIP LEADS, & ELECTRONIC ACCESSORIES	100.00
ELECTRONIC HANDBOOKS	40.00

TOTAL - 340.50

TOTAL p. 1 & 2 - $1178.50

Fig 05

Fig 06

Gita Sarabhai, who was perhaps still eager to understand the influence of Western music.

For the first two weeks, Tudor gave lectures and guided the students through the workings of the Moog before moving on to individual sessions to develop what each participant wanted to do. Interestingly, one photo taken at the class shows him holding a vinyl record of the *Extended Voices* LP, containing his earlier attempt to subvert the possibilities of the same synthesizer [see page 20]. Joshipura also remembered the "little boxes" of his own that Tudor brought along, which he would connect to the Moog and play around.[34] Towards the end of his stay, Tudor organized a performance at the lawn of NID where he played a three-hour-long tape that he had put together from the materials his students had composed. He gave a befitting title to the fortuitous event which is said to have attracted a huge audience: *Incidental Music*.

7

Whenever Tudor looked back at this visit in the later years, however, it was not *Incidental Music* that he recalled, but a particular incidental music he had to make for the occasion. In his telling of the story, it was Gita Sarabhai who asked him to organize an event at NID to present the music she had made with the Moog. But when he made all the arrangements to make this concert happen, Gita suddenly got stage fright. From what he remembered in 1984: "I was very unhappy when I've gone to great trouble to arrange for Gita to present her compositions and she chickened out. She was afraid. It wasn't good enough. And so I just had to be satisfied by the fact that it would never be good enough."[35] Having set up a performance situation with no performance, Tudor decided to take matters into his own hands: "I had to make a piece, and the only thing available was this synthesizer. So I put all my gain stages into a single oscillator [laughing] and the poor thing doesn't know what it's doing. It turned out to be fun, eventually."[36]

What Tudor had done was to apply his method of connecting instruments in a feedback loop to create signals at many points within the circuit through their mismatch and influence. Adding the little boxes of his own in the mix would have certainly helped to disrupt the otherwise

→ Fig 07

T: Oh you bet. I use the synthesizer in performance for one piece or another, I mean, for instance John Cage's "Variations VI." We had that and "Variations VII." We had that as part of the pot, but make a piece, and a, I had to make a piece, and the only thing available was this synthesizer. So I put all my gainstages into a single oscillator (laughing) and the poor thing doesn't know what it's doing. It turned out to be fun, eventually.

refers to MONOBIRD, made in 69 (Ahmedabad) elaborated in 72 for Munich

F:Your image 'the lay of the land.' It's that you're exploring, crawling around in the machines?

T: Yes. Well, I don't like to tell the machines what to do. It's when they do something that I didn't know about, and I can help it along, then all of a sudden I know the piece is mine. Otherwise, you set out to make a scale of pitches or a scale of dynamics; anybody can do that.

F: That isn't much fun. The best that happens is you'll succeed.

T: (laughing) Yes. And if you don't succeed you'll be disappointed.

F: Right.

T: It's much better to be surprised.

F: When you're working on either a new piece or on a performance of a piece you've done before when you're setting the piece up, it's going to be different. How do you know when to quit setting up; when is it ready to fly?

T: Well, there are lots of ways of handling things. A lot depends on how elaborate the output situation is. For instance, if I have the chance to expand the output, then I may be busying myself with splitting my output. You know, so that instead of having one auxiliary channel I might have two channels or three channels or four channels and each one of those is like a different procedure, so I could stop without doing that, but I can continue, so it's fun to do that.

On the other hand there's the opposite proposition, where for instance if the components are lacking then you decide what the essential thing is that's supposed to happen and do it with whatever is available. I mean, that's happened to me, when the freight didn't arrive and you're stuck with a mixer and a cassette recorder; you have a figure out what to do. (laughter)

F: Right. The permutations are fewer though.

T: My group had an interesting time when we were at I guess it was the Kitchen, and we wanted to work together, but we sort of didn't.. None of us was willing to really make a group piece. So we decided to perform as a group with the pieces that we each had. I had my "Forest Speech" which is a variation of "Rainforest." And I gave them the block diagram of that and Ralph Jones had a piece.. he gave us his block diagrams, John Driscoll and Martin Kalve, and so there we were. I believe Driscoll was the only *Component* one who had any duplicates which he could give us to use, and even that was only just the smallest part of what he was asking for. But everyone realised the predictable and nonfortuitous nature of the commercial synthesizer he had delivered. The use of feedback through a single oscillator is also supported by the sound of the recording Tudor made using the Moog synthesizer, which repeats the same short pattern of sine-wave-like chirps going up and down which is gradually shifted as Tudor manipulates the control here and there. The sound indeed reminds one of bird songs characterized by what ornithologists call "syllables," short segments of repeated patterns that birds are known to learn and perform through auditory feedback. As Paul Purgas's research revealed, the reel-to-reel tape-recording Tudor made at NID[37] was labelled "BIRDS," with the words "Mono" inscribed (and scribbled out) next to it in parenthesis to indicate the fact that it was a monaural recording. A short note Tudor wrote down in the margins of the transcript of the 1984 interview has revealed the title Tudor gave to this recording: "refers to MONOBIRD, made in 69 (Ahmedabad) elaborated in 72 for Munich."[38] [FIG 07] Tudor would go on to use this incidental music throughout the 1970s.[39]

8

But one wonders why Gita became afraid. Perhaps her concern for the influence of Western music on the traditional music of her country persisted in her mind. The two extant tapes that Gita created using the Moog synthesizer offer a glimpse into what she might have intended.[40] One is a 45-minute stereo recording of experiments in electronic sound processing that is segmented into five parts.[41] The other is a 20-minute collection of pitches of a chromatic scale played with square and sine wave tones. However, the latter follows idiosyncratic intervals which appear to be Gita's deliberate effort to simulate not the Western equal temperament scale but *swaras*, the traditional scale of Indian music, something that the specification in parenthesis added to the description on the case of the reel tape also suggests: "Frequencies in Square and Sine Wave of Chromatic Scale (Indian)."[42] Moreover, towards the end of the same tape, short recordings of Indian music played in reverse are twice dubbed onto the monaural recording (at 13:25 and 18:25), a feature that resonates with the final part of the other recording which happens to be a sitar performance (from 39:40). All in all, there seems to be an attempt to impose the influence of her country's music onto an instrument that could have behaved otherwise. Perhaps this was a far-reaching consequence of

Gita's incidental exchange with Cage so many years before. But influences are notoriously difficult to analyze, let alone control.

9

Cage wrote in 1954 that his understanding of music's purpose and divine influence had come from the Indian tradition through his learning with Gita. But in a lecture given on February 28, 1948—just a year after Gita left—he attributed a completely different origin to the same teaching:

> To what end does one write music? Fortunately I did not need to face this question alone. Lou Harrison, and now Merton Brown, another composer and close friend, were always ready to talk and ask and discuss any question relative to music with me. We began to read the works of Ananda K. Coomaraswamy and we met Gita Sarabhai, who came like an angel from India. She was a traditional musician and told us that her teacher had said that the purpose of music was to concentrate the mind. Lou Harrison found a passage by Thomas Mace written in England in 1676 to the effect that the purpose of music was to season and sober the mind, thus making it susceptible of divine influences, and elevating one's affections to goodness.[43]

Indeed, the proverb Cage would later claim as having delivered by "an angel from India," turns out to be a phrase composed by mixing sentences from *Musick's Monument*, a treatise written by a seventeenth-century English composer and lutenist: ""[T]o Season, and Sober his Mind, or Elevate his Affection to Goodness" comes from one passage, and "[M]aking us capable of Heavenly, and Divine Influence" comes from another.'[44] As Austin Clarkson notes, Thomas Mace, in his lifetime, was closely associated with the Cambridge Platonists, a group of philosophers immersed in the tradition of mysticism going all the way back to Neo-Platonism by way of Renaissance magic and astrology. No wonder his teaching placed its emphasis on the power of music to render the listener susceptible to external influences. In other words, this lesson shared its history with anthroposophy, rooted in the tradition of esotericism that Tudor understood all too well.

Thus, the tradition Gita went a long way to protect may have been infiltrated by Western influence from the beginning. Or more probably, Cage had relocated the origin of this traditional reason for making music from old England to old India in his retelling of the story, thereby filtering out any trace of Western influence and amplifying the flair of exotic authenticity to his learning. Steiner would not have been happy. In the 1954 lecture, Cage simply dismissed the transposition as an incidental affair:

Same answer is given by some old
English composer. *Consider this non-dualistically.*[45]

But if Cage's account of what Gita brought from India is dubious, what about his account of why she came over in the first place? Was it really her who was concerned about the influence of Western music? The answer to these questions probably lies (if at all) in the private archives of the Sarabhai family. In any case, a tradition was fabricated—and just like Tudor's karma that accelerated through his connection to anthroposophy, the influence of this tradition would have far-reaching consequences, some of them quite fortuitous for some individuals more than others.

10

In April 1970, four months after Tudor's departure, Lowell Cross arrived in Ahmedabad. He did not have to fly all the way across the Pacific Ocean, as he had just been in Japan, working with Tudor on the Pepsi Pavilion project for the Osaka Expo which had opened its doors in mid-March of that year. This was an endeavor organized by Experiments in Art and Technology (E.A.T.), a non-profit group based in New York dedicated to fostering the collaboration between artists and engineers. Although Joshipura recalled Tudor being announced as the director of E.A.T., he was only a member of the same group and E.A.T. was not officially part of his residency at NID. But there was a concern to frame it as if it were, partly on the side of NID who wanted to promote the importance of their guest lecturer, partly on the side of the Sarabhais who were eager to invite more American artists through the portal of NID, and partly on the side of E.A.T. who wanted to expand their activities further westward after their adventures in Japan.

On November 17, 1969, while Tudor was still giving classes in Ahmedabad, Gira Sarabhai wrote to Billy Klüver, the real director of E.A.T., in response to a plan they had been offered in connection to the upcoming project in relatively nearby Japan:

> We have had discussions with David and he has given us a list of the participants at E.A.T. Pavilion in Osaka. Much as we would be interested in initiating a joint project with E.A.T., in which artists, engineers and others who will be at the E.A.T. Pavilion at Osaka, come to NID to work on a given project, the main problem at our end is finance. [...] There are, however, certain people in whom we are greatly interested. [...] For our sound studio, David feels it would be very useful to have Lowell Cross. Lowell could teach sound recording and maintenance of equipment at professional level. As a musician, he could continue the work which David has started.[46]

When Lowell Cross came half a year later, it was as the first artist of the "American Artists in India" program that E.A.T. had launched with a grant from the John D. Rockefeller III Fund. Over the course of the next eighteen months, seven more artists would follow Gita's trajectory from a quarter-century before in reverse, relocating temporarily from New York to India for cultural exchange—to learn and to be influenced.[47]

11

One of the participants in the program was the choreographer Yvonne Rainer who travelled across the subcontinent for six weeks in January and February 1971. She kept a journal of her journey where she documented her impression of many Indian theater, dance, and music performances she encountered.[48] The choreographer went back to New York disillusioned about her own works, entertaining fantasies of giving up dance. Instead, she started working on a strange piece reflecting her experiences in India, which was neither dance nor theater but something in between. In May of that year, she presented the new work which she titled *Grand Union Dreams*. This was the first performance in which Rainer set characters for her performers who were cast in one of the three categories of roles: Mortals, Heroes, and Gods. When asked about her choices she answered, "That came after seeing a lot of theater in India."[49] Critics called the piece "her most problematic work."[50] Soon after this piece Rainer stopped making dance and became a filmmaker. Thirty-five years later, I became very interested in an American choreographer named Yvonne Rainer, and especially in a strange theater/dance she had made in 1971. So, in 2007, I decided to fly to Los Angeles from Tokyo to interview Rainer about *Grand Union Dreams*, which she tried to remember but could no longer gather many of the details. She told me that her materials had recently been moved to the Getty Research Institute and suggested I go there. When I contacted the Getty, they replied saying that Rainer's materials were in their archive, but they were still being processed so I could not see them. They informed me that I can nevertheless visit the special collections room if I wished. I looked up what else they have in store and quite fortuitously came across the David Tudor Papers which I didn't know existed. So, I ordered several boxes and took a day trip to the Getty Research Institute on November 8, 2007, only to be astonished by the number of materials Tudor had left behind—including a recording of one strange music that he had incidentally made almost forty years before in an Indian city named Ahmedabad.

* I would like to thank Paul Purgas and Alexander Keefe for their pioneering research as well as for sharing the materials they collected when the COVID-19 pandemic made it impossible to conduct archival research in Ahmedabad.

Notes

1 John Cage, "Afternote to *Lecture on Nothing*," in *Silence* (Middletown, CT: Wesleyan University, 1961), 127.

2 Ibid.

3   Ibid.

4   Before she left, Gita gave Cage the English translation of Mahendranath Gupta, *The Gospel of Sri Ramakrishna*, which he recalls spending a year to finish reading. (Ibid.)

5   Story 79 in John Cage and David Tudor, *Indeterminacy: New Aspect of Form in Instrumental and Electronic Music. Ninety Stories by John Cage, with Music.* Folkways FT 3704, 1959. Reissued as Smithsonian/Folkways CD DF 40804/5, 1992. Variation in Cage, "Afternote to *Lecture on Nothing*."

6   For instance, see: David W. Patterson, "Cage and Asia: History and Sources," in David Nicholls (ed.), *The Cambridge Companion to John Cage* (Cambridge: Cambridge University Press, 2002), 48–49.

7   John Cage, "45" for a Speaker" in *Silence*, 158. He later elucidated: "A sober and quiet mind is one in which the ego does not obstruct the fluency of things that come in through the senses and up through our dreams. Our business in living is to become fluent with the life we are living, and art can help this." (Cage, "Memoir," in Richard Kostelanetz, John Cage (London: Allen Lane, 1971), 77. He would repeat this story until the end of his life. See, for instance: John Cage, "An Autobiographical Statement." John Cage Trust, 1990, http://johncage.org/autobiographical_statement.html.

8   Incidentally, the provenance of the other proverb was also—at least seemingly—India, as it was derived from the reading of Ananda K. Coomaraswamy's *The Transformation of Art in Nature* (1934), a study of oriental aesthetic theory based mainly on Indian sources: "The function of art is to imitate nature in her manner of operation." However, in reading Coomaraswamy's book, one realizes that this formula is actually a quote from Thomas Aquinas which the author presents as also applying to Indian art: "for the East, as for St Thomas, *ars imitatur naturam in sua operatione*." (*The Transformation of Art in Nature,* New York: Dover Publications, 1956, 15) For a detailed inquiry into the manner of operation of Cage's works using this proverb as a key of sorts, see: Nakai, "How to Imitate Nature in Her Manner of Operation: Between What John Cage Did and What He Said He Did," *Perspectives of New Music*, Vol. 52, No. 3 (Autumn 2014), 141–160.

9   David Tudor, "Letter to M.C. Richards (October 20, 1958)," Folder 2 Box 26, Mary Caroline Richards papers, Getty Research Institute.

10   David Tudor, "Letter to M.C. Richards (October 28, 1958)," Folder 2 Box 26, Mary Caroline Richards papers, Getty Research Institute.

11   Robert Rauschenberg Oral History Project, "The Reminiscences of Asha and Suhrid Sarabhai," Columbia Center for Oral History Research, 2015, 15.

12   David Tudor, "Letter to M.C. Richards (November 28, 1961)," Folder 2 Box 26, Mary Caroline Richards papers, Getty Research Institute.

13   Manorama Sarabhai, "Letter to David Tudor (August 10, 1965)," Folder 3 Box 59, David Tudor Papers, Getty Research Institute.

14   David Tudor, "Letter to M.C. Richards (October 25, 1962)," Folder 2 Box 26, Mary Caroline Richards Papers, Getty Research Institute.

15   For a detailed study of Theosophy's expansion in India, see: Hans Martin Krämer and Julian Strube (eds.), *Theosophy across Boundaries: Transcultural and Interdisciplinary Perspectives on a Modern Esoteric Movement* (Albany, NY: SUNY Press, 2020); Peter van der Veer, *Imperial Encounters: Religion and Modernity in India and Britain* (Princeton, NJ: Princeton University Press, 2001), 55–82; and John L. Crow, "Taming the Astral Body: The Theosophical Society's Ongoing Problem of Emotion and Control," *Journal of the American Academy of Religion*, Vol. 80, No. 3 (September 2012), 691–717.

16   For an example of Steiner's diatribe against these external influences: "The European civilisation had lost any spiritual power, and that is why the big stimulations had to come from the East at first. Hence, the word: ex oriente lux.—Then however, when this light had come, one found the spark again, so that also in Europe the religious confessions could be kindled. Today we do not in the least need to adhere to the reminiscences of Buddhism. Today we are able to show the matter absolutely from our European culture, from the Christian culture without pointing to Buddhist springs or origins or other oriental influence." (*Steiner, Spiritual Teachings of Soul/World: Course V—Lecture IV: Is Theosophy Buddhist Propaganda?*)

17   For instance, see: Rudolf Steiner, *Planetary Spheres and Their Influence on Man's Life on Earth and in the Spiritual Worlds* (London, UK: Rudolf Steiner Press, 1982). For a fascinating account on the revival of Neo-Platonism via the (mis)translation of *Corpus Hermeticum* by Marsilio Ficino in 1471, and all the consequent turn of events, see: Frances Yates, *Giordano Bruno and the Hermetic Tradition* (Chicago, IL: University of Chicago Press, 1964).

18   Tudor, "From Piano to Electronics," 26.

19   Ray Wilding-White, "David Tudor: 10 Selected Realizations of Graphic Scores and Related Performances (1974)," Box 19, Folder 2, David Tudor Papers, GRI.

20   Alvin Lucier, "Interview by You Nakai," April 22, 2017, Middletown, CT.

21   A.R. Mehta, "Letter to David Tudor (March 15, 1968)," Folder 2 Box 59, David Tudor Papers, Getty Research Institute.

22   Robert Moog, "Letter to David Tudor (October 22, 1965)," Box 41, David Tudor Papers, GRI. This device may or may not have been delivered. If Tudor did obtain it, the instrument's subsequent use and whereabouts are unknown.

23   "An Interview with David Tudor by John David Fullemann in Stockholm, May 31, 1984," davidtudor.org, accessed December 15, 2021: http://davidtudor.org/Articles/fullemann.html. Although the interview is dated May 31, this cannot be correct since Tudor was nowhere near Sweden on that day. Fullemann talks about "the performance last night" at the start of the interview, which he clarifies as referring to Tudor's concert of *Dialects* at the Moderna Museet in Stockholm. Tudor indeed performed *Dialects* in

Stockholm in 1984, but that was on September 2, which reveals the interview to have taken place the following day: September 3.

24   Gnazzo, "Email to John Bischoff," March 3, 2015. Alden Jenks, who was a student there, similarly recalled how his teacher "killed the Buchla dead": "I do remember that he sat down in front of the Buchla system one evening. [...] David proceeded to grab a handful of cords and, with a sort of devilish smile, very rapidly set the lights in motion in a complex pattern until, with one final connection, the whole thing suddenly stopped—he had forced the machine to turn itself off." (Alden Jenks, "Email to You Nakai," March 13, 2015.)

25   Mumma, "Email interview by You Nakai," March 5, 2016.

26   Mumma, "Interview by Nakai," November 11, 2016. To the question of how they had access to Moog instruments, he reminisced: "Well, we may have borrowed something. I don't remember what it was. Moog also had some modules that we would change back and forth. I think I traded some of them with my own. You know, simple stuff. There was nothing complex. These were sort of sound effects things that we used for *Solos for Voice*." (Ibid.)

27   Meanwhile, there was one person who must have been very happy about the whole deal and that was Robert Moog himself. In an article titled "Moog Music is Here to Stay," published on September 7, 1969, in the "Music and the Arts" section of the *St. Louis Post-Dispatch*, writer Frank Peters praised Moog's synthesizer as having "made a breakthrough that electronic music has been waiting for all these years," comparing it to the long lineage of electronic instruments "right up to the sophisticated Syn-Ket of our own decade," which "had their day in the sun [...] but none took root." As evidence of the breakthrough, the article mentioned "There are more than 200 Moog Synthesizers in the world today, nearly all of them sold in the last two years, and new ones are being bought as fast as universities and studios can scrape up the purchase money. An elementary school in Philadelphia has one for pupil use. So does the University of Jerusalem and the National Design Institute of India." (Frank Peters, "Music and the Arts," *St. Louis Post-Dispatch* (September 7, 1969); Folder 9 Box 37, David Tudor Papers, Getty Research Institute).

28   Manorama Sarabhai, "Letter to David Tudor (March 1, 1969)," Folder 3 Box 59, David Tudor Papers, Getty Research Institute.

29   For instance, the inquiry on August 4, 1969, concerned an equipment for visualizing sound: "I am enclosing with this letter the complete specifications of Oscilloscope No. 481-I model manufactured by Simson ElectronicCo. in India. This particular instrument is readily available. It comes very near the specifications of the instrument already selected by you. May I ask you to drop me a line if the Oscilloscope's specifications meet your approval. It was a pleasure speaking to you over the telephone today." (J. Anand,

"Letter to David Tudor (August 4, 1969)," Folder 1 Box 59, David Tudor Papers, Getty Research Institute).

30   R.A. Moog, "Schematics for synthesizer modules," Box 3 Folder 39, David Tudor Papers, Getty Research Institute.

31   This photograph was taken circa 2012 by Dhun Kakaria, who purchased the equipment when NID was ready to let it go. I thank Alexander Keefe for kindly sharing this material with me.

32   Photographs of many corresponding extant instruments can be seen online at: http://remindedbytheinstruments.info (access: January 20, 2022). Especially notable are two substitution boxes that allowed switching between different values of resistors and capacitors which Tudor often used with the AA-100 Amplifiers also listed here, inserting the substitution boxes in the feedback path around the amplifier to create a composite oscillator. He had used this configuration as input in his *Rainforest* performances and described it as making animal-like or bird-like sounds. For more detail on these Rainforest Amplifiers, see: Nakai, "Appendix B: Rainforest Amplifiers," in *Reminded by the Instruments: David Tudor's Music* (New York, NY: Oxford University Press, 2021).

33   Jinraj Joshipura, "Interview by You Nakai," Zoom, January 28, 2022.

34   Ibid.

35   "An Interview with David Tudor by John David Fullemann in Stockholm, May 31, 1984," davidtudor.org, accessed December 15, 2021: http://davidtudor.org/Articles/fullemann.html.

36   Ibid. In another interview from 1985, Tudor again described what he had done in more detail: "All of a sudden I had to make something. So I took a couple of hours and I made a synthesizer piece. [...] I decided that I better find a way to tweak it out. I had already done a little experimenting with the early Buchla synthesizer, and a very nice technique was to load a mixer up and put it in a feedback loop. So I decided to take a single oscillator and load up all its control inputs and sure enough, you would think there would be thirty oscillators but there is only one."

37   David Tudor, "Duplicate taken from David's composition tape BIRDS," T430, National Design Institute archives.

38   But there is something different about the original *Birds* tape left in the archives of NID from the *Monobird* tapes that Tudor took back to New York and used as material for performances throughout the next decade. The former contains an overdub of someone laughing towards the beginning. It turns out that these laughter sounds are from the dancer Chandralekha which Tudor had recorded and mixed with his Birds music made on Moog. According to how cultural critic Sadanand Menon told it, the intended effect was contagion through influence: "One evening at the NID lawns, as people assembled for an event, David Tudor had recorded Chandra's bubbly laughter

and serially relayed it through ten directional speakers so that the laughter "traveled" and infected everyone and the entire assembly started laughing." (Sadanand Menon, quoted in Alexander Keefe, "E-mail to You Nakai," February 10, 2022).

38   For a detailed history of *Monobird*, see You Nakai, "When David Tudor Went Disco: The No-Audience Laser Concert Without the Laser at Xenon," booklet accompanying the double LP, David Tudor, *Monobirds: From Ahmedabad to Xenon* (TOPOS, 2021).

39   Gita Mayor, "Gitaben's composition on Moog electronic synthesizes [sic] under the guidance of David Tudor," T509, National Design Institute archives; Geeta Mayor, "Frequencies in Square and Sine Wave of Chromatic Scale (Indian)," T445, National Design Institute archive. I thank Paul Purgas for generously sharing with me these two recordings.

41   The division of sections are as follows: 07:15, 23:58, 37:50, 39:35.

42   The pitches and their corresponding tuning in cents are: C-C# (100)-D (200)-D# (275)-E (370)-F (475)-F# (575)-G (730)-G# (775)-A (885)-A# (955)-B (1055) for sine wave; and B-C (100)-C# (200)-D (310)-D# (380)-E (485)-F (585)-F# (685)-G (785)-G# (885)-A (980)-A# (1055)-B (1140) for square wave.

43   John Cage, "A Composer's Confessions (1948)," in, Richard Kostelanetz (ed.), *John Cage: Writer* (New York, NY: Cooper Square Press, 2000), 41. Although given in 1948, the original text of this lecture was not published until 1992.

44   Austin Clarkson, "The Intent of the Musical Moment," in David W. Bernstein and Christopher Hatch (eds.), *Writing Through John Cage's Music, Poetry + Art* (Chicago, IL: The University of Chicago Press, 2001), 79.

45   Cage, "45" for a Speaker" in *Silence*, 158.

46   Gira Sarabhai, "Letter to Billy Klüver (November 17, 1969)," Folder 1 Box 17, David Tudor Papers, Getty Research Institute.

47   They were Terry Riley, Trisha Brown, Jed Bark, Yvonne Rainer, Jeffrey Lew, La Monte Young and Marion Zazeela.

48   Yvonne Rainer, "India Journal," in *Work 1961-73* (New York, NY: New York University Press, 1974), 173–188.

49   Yvonne Rainer, "Grand Union Dreams," in *Work 1961-73* (New York, NY: New York University Press, 1974), 191.

50   Annette Michelson, "Yvonne Rainer, Part Two; "Lives of Performers,"" *Artforum*, February 1974, 30.

ELECTRONIC INDIA: ORIGINS
Geeta Dayal

The electronic music studio in Ahmedabad, founded in 1969, didn't emerge out of nowhere. It was part of a continuum. In various parts of India in the 1960s, ideas from science fiction, outer space exploration, and psychedelic rock were beginning to permeate the popular consciousness. Electronic instruments were entering the landscape. In Bollywood cinema, the visionary composer and music director R.D. Burman pioneered the use of electric organs in the 1966 song "O Mere Sona Re," years before the Bollywood electronic disco and funk of the 1970s and 1980s.

For many of the Western rock bands and celebrities who visited India in the 1960s, the India they sought was an ancient one, a bygone land that exists primarily in the mind. They were seeking truth and history, via gurus, mystical temples, yoga and Eastern philosophies. They were looking for something deeper and more timeless than what they knew—an escape from the overt materialism of Western culture. The ambassadors of Indian culture to the West, most famously Ravi Shankar, further reinforced these notions. Indian music would forever be associated, in the Western mind, with Indian classical music, via the cosmic thrum of the sitar.

Meanwhile, during the same era, many in India were seeking exactly the opposite. They were interested in synthesizers and electric guitars, not harmoniums and sitars. They were searching for the future, not the past.

← Suresh Shottam of The Spartans. Bristol Beat Contest, Bengaluru, 1968.

India celebrated its hard-fought independence in 1947, and the future was bright. Space exploration got an early start on the subcontinent. In 1962, the Indian National Committee for Space Research (INCOSPAR) was established by Jawaharlal Nehru and prominent scientists including Vikram Sarabhai, the brother of Gita and Gira Sarabhai. By late 1963, India had launched its first rocket into sub-orbital space from Thumba, a village in Kerala. Science fiction was percolating too. In 1965, in the pages of the Bengali children's magazine *Sandesh*, the legendary film director Satyajit Ray was quietly inventing radical new sci-fi through the adventures of his wily protagonist, Professor Shonku. That year, Ray published a story in *Sandesh* which envisioned a futuristic electronic musical contraption called a "microsonograph" used by Shonku. The device could record and amplify sounds that were inaudible to humans. In 1967, Ray wrote a movie script called *The Alien*, about a spaceship landing in a village in West Bengal.

Space rock and psychedelic rock bands were also forming in India, though they tended to sound low-fi, partly for reasons of equipment. Electronic music and psychedelic rock both rely heavily on gear. To transport a listener to another plane, it helped to craft a novel sonic environment.

In India, much of this gear wasn't readily accessible. That's part of the reason why electronic music didn't proliferate as quickly in the late 1960s and early 1970s as it did in the West, and why the rock music from that era in Bombay sounds like garage rock. (A few bands like Atomic Forest, which had a heavier vibe, got closer to psychedelia, splitting the difference between psych-rock and Black Sabbath-style metal.) In the book *India Psychedelic*, on the hidden history of rock in India in the 1960s and early 1970s, Siddharth Bhatia quotes a despairing article on the state of Indian rock music from the British rock paper *NME* in 1973: "Putting together a rock band in India, bless their chapatis, is much akin to bashing one's head against a brick wall. It's painful—and the result is negative."

India was treading very different social, political, and economic waters than the West. "The swinging '60s that swept Britain and the West in general barely trickled in here," Bhatia writes. "India was too busy trying to survive. It was a testing time for a young nation as it struggled to cope with overwhelming odds...India lurched from crisis to crisis, each one more severe than the previous one."

Several major rock bands from the West visited India in the 1960s and 1970s. But these famous groups didn't tour in India; the Beatles didn't do much to nurture India's music scenes when they visited Maharishi Mahesh Yogi's ashram in Rishikesh. (Apple Records did reach out, at one point, to the Calcutta band The Flintstones, but The Flintstones had mostly disbanded, and apparently didn't answer.) "The Beatles, Led Zep and Donovan came to India but in their private capacities and did not hold any concerts," Bhatia writes. "The US State Department had brought famous jazz musicians like Louis Armstrong, Dave Brubeck and Duke Ellington to India as part of cultural diplomacy and propaganda, but no government sponsored the visit of a rock group." Jimmy Page and Robert Plant of Led Zeppelin did play one gig in Bombay in 1972, in a small venue, on a night that still mostly remains shrouded in mystery.

Electric guitars were hard to find, and the guitars that were available in India were often less than optimal (Bhatia hilariously describes the "Givson", an Indian guitar brand modelled on the Gibson.) When you hear a band like the Velvette Fogg heroically attempting to cover Cream's hit "I'm So Glad," especially when they try to nail Eric Clapton's guitar solo and massive sound with a guitar tone that sounds like rusty tin cans, you have to smile. It sounds like it was recorded through a cardboard tube, and that's part of the music's inherent charm. Compared to the over-the-top richness of Bollywood filmi music, Indian rock from the 1960s sounds positively minimalist—appealingly rough, and refreshing in its proto-punk simplicity. Sonically, the Velvette Fogg had more in common with the Velvet Underground than they did with Cream, and that's not a bad thing.

Sometimes having less to work with can motivate creative solutions. In Germany, bands in the burgeoning "Krautrock" scene in the late 1960s and 1970s often made do by modifying existing instruments, repurposing military surplus equipment, or employing various found objects. The great German group Can, for example, wrapped huge tape loops around beer bottles while making their 1971 album *Tago Mago*. Bhatia describes one Indian band where three band members huddled around one reverb unit. Another musician had to heat up his leather drum to make it playable, because the humidity would cause it to sag.

One way for Indian bands to get around the dearth of guitars and other Western instruments was to use traditional Indian instruments too, just as many Western bands were appropriating Indian instruments into their rock music. Human Bondage, one of the more successful Indian bands (the name, of course, is a wry W. Somerset Maugham reference), merged traditional Indian instrumentation with guitars, integrating instruments like the dholak into a potent "raga rock" mix. This appears to have never been recorded, along with most of Human Bondage's output. You can't hear much of what the band did, because they never released a full LP, despite their popularity.

That raises an issue even more pressing than the relative lack of gear—the fact that there isn't a massive recorded legacy of Indian rock and electronic music from that time. There aren't piles and piles of full-length albums. The recordings that exist are scattered, in a large part because the entire infrastructure of these scenes also didn't really exist in India. The Simla Beat Contest, the famed competition in Bombay that brought together Indian rock bands, and *Junior Statesman*, a magazine that covered the scene, were notable exceptions to the rule. For the most part, there wasn't a collection of record labels, record stores, radio stations, and venues in India in the 1960s and 1970s to support the careers of these young artists. It wasn't just difficult to find the local albums; it was often hard to find the major albums from abroad, too.

In this young country with an ancient history, full of ideas, hope and fitful beginnings, we sometimes wonder what could have been. What if Ray's script for *The Alien* had been made, and it became a Hollywood blockbuster? What if we had many more albums from these Indian psychedelic rock bands? It is a small miracle that the vintage electronic Moog recordings from Ahmedabad exist, and that we can now listen to them. In this inspiring music, we hear bold new pathways for the future.

See With Your Ears
Alannah Chance

The start of any documentary for a radio producer is a bit dizzying. You do your research, you make the calls, you draw up your questions, but once the recorder is switched on it's a dance between preparation and chance. The story of the birth of electronic music in India was similar, a chance operation birthed through sound, silence and happy accidents. It's also, in many ways, a story which shouldn't have happened. The Moog was brought to Ahmedabad by David Tudor, a pianist and a purist who disliked the way synthesisers operated. Equally the National Institute of Design (NID) was a design school rather than a music school so the students weren't necessarily predisposed to make use of its multi-wired complexities. Timing wise it was not fortuitous either. It crash landed at a pivotal point in the history of post-independence India, when the priorities of the new nation were still undecided.

But we didn't know that back then, as Paul Purgas and I battled through the chaos of cars and cattle in Ahmedabad, assembling recording gear on the back seat of a taxi. We were there to make a radio documentary for BBC Radio 3 called *Electronic India*[1], uncovering the unlikely story of the Moog at the NID and trying to track down the remaining composers who worked on it. Paul had discovered a box of reel-to-reel tapes from the institute's archive, featuring a series of unknown composers experimenting with early synthesis. It changed the timeline on the history of electronic music, often misguidedly western-centric, adding an Indian chapter as early as the late 1960s.

← Gautum Gira Sarabhai Square at the NID.

I remember when I first heard the tapes with Paul on the NID campus. The tape was a fragile, membrane-thin ribbon, patched together with peeling yellow sellotape. Paul sat and painstakingly reassembled it, fragment by fragment, and placed it on the reel-to-reel player. As a dedicated radio producer I turned off the air-con and in the muggy silence we hit record. A clunk, a whirl and a hiss and the machine lurched into life. Then a disembodied voice with the clipped vowels of the 60s began to talk. It was a recording of a radio programme on All India Radio discussing the history of electronic music in India. It pre-dated my own attempts on the same subject 50 years later and featured the NID composers Atul Desai, sound engineer I.S. Mathur alongside the designer Vikas Satwalekar who, when asked what he thinks about electronic music, says: "You can hear with your eyes and see with your ears...and why not."

The NID's main campus is situated on a main road in the heart of Ahmedabad, lined with vendors selling sim cards and puri stacked in hand carts. After stepping into the grounds the car horns and hustle of the streets fall away as you emerge onto a large lawn ringed by trees, the wide concrete balconies of the NID looming through the leaves. The institute has changed a lot since it was established in 1961 but a spirit of openness remains. We met one student from the original intake in the 1960s, a former designer now in his 80s, who still comes to the library every day to read and watch the swallows swoop over the grounds at dusk.

Deepankar Bhattacharyya, a designer who arrived in 1970, explained the NID's approach to education: "We didn't have grades, nobody was marking you vis-à-vis someone else. They were not really interested in getting the student to learn a specified set of things, they were more interested in developing a student's ability to interface with what education is all about." The intake in the early years was small, there were only around 25 students in his year and students were all on first name terms with the staff, unheard of in India at that time. Progress wasn't marked through grades or delivering projects but through an undefined demonstration of personal growth. This hands-on approach was led by Gautam Sarabhai himself: "When I finished I was very confused about what I was going to do. I called up Gautam Sarabhai and we spent a couple of hours sitting on the lawn at dusk. Birds would come home to roost at that time and he started off by asking me to listen to the bird sounds, watch the birds, look at the setting sun, to feel the breeze...and then we started to talk about what design wasn't, and how you really need to look at design through a sensory apparatus, rather than any sort of mental thing. You did it through your eyes and your ears and through emotions. It did give me a great deal of clarity."

In the 1960s the NID's approach to education was led by the Sarabhai family, primarily the siblings Gira and Gautam Sarabhai, who drew from a diverse pool of pedagogical influences that included Montessori, the Bauhaus, Shantiniketan in India as well as the democratic school Summerhill in the UK. Funding from the Ford Foundation allowed them to bring over the latest equipment and the Sarabhais' impressive list of contacts helped draw notable guest artists and designers from the US and Europe, including Frei Otto, Henri Cartier-Bresson, Stella Kramrisch and Robert Rauschenberg.

While Gautam led on the NID's approach to education, it was another of his sisters, Gita, herself a musician, who helped bring the Moog to the institute. Gita and Cage had become close, exchanging notes on music while she was living in New York and he in turn had visited the NID on more than one occasion (with Merce Cunningham and Robert Rauschenberg as well as David Tudor). Tudor had partly brought the Moog over under the auspices of E.A.T. (Experiments in Art and Technology), a New York based arts organisation dedicated to connecting artists and engineers. While at the NID he had given workshops on the Moog, including to Gita, whose name we found on a few of the tapes. I tried to track down any remaining members of the family for the documentary but was told that the Sarabhais had become reclusive since retiring from their position in 1973.

Then, on our last day in Ahmedabad, I received a text out of the blue from Gita Sarabhai's grandson Ajay. His mother Pallavi, the daughter of Gita, was happy to meet us. He invited us to their villa in the suburbs, adjacent to Le Corbusier's famous Villa Sarabhai. We arrived at the top of the drive and were ushered into the front room, and settled on low cushions alongside their labrador. There Pallavi Mayor recounted what she remembered of those days: "Gandhi's ashram was a stone's throw from here and they used to go to his prayer meetings. All the people who came to the ashram would stay with my grandparents. So these kids grew up with all these wonderful guests in the house."

Gita was predominantly an Indian classical vocalist and percussionist, and as Pallavi explained, was a respected figure within the community.

"My mother had an immense understanding of music. She would be sitting in the audience and musicians would address her from stage because she was considered a connoisseur. She had a tremendous passion and interest in Indian music right to the end. In her 80s and 90s if there was a concert, even at 12 o'clock at night she would want to go." Gita Sarabhai had a conviction that the purpose of music was to calm the mind and according to Pallavi "that really made a huge impression on John Cage". But of the electronic music that Gita produced on the Moog, Pallavi had no memory. We found two tapes in the NID collection where you can hear Gita experimenting with the synthesizer but other than that, as far as we know, she had not composed any works on it that survived.

This was a common theme across the Moog tapes. Listening to the pieces themselves, there's a sense of play during the early period, of people feeling out the boundaries of the instrument. The pieces were named "Birds", "Bubbles" and "Moogsical Forms" as they played with ideas for radio jingles and sound effects for films. There are also more composed pieces, "Dance Music" by NID studio engineer S.C. Sharma was one of them, a piece of proto-techno which wouldn't sound out of place 20 years later in Detroit, and Jinraj Joshipura's soundtrack opus "Space Liner 2001". Joshipura being the only remaining composer we were able to track down for the programme to hear his incredible story. After Tudor installed the Moog in 1969 with a few accompanying workshops, there's no more tuition on the instrument. From this point onwards the students and faculty on the tapes are experimenting solo, free from any expectation of what electronic music should be. It's this spirit of pure experimentation that makes these pieces sing. It's experimental music in the truest sense.

This is a common theme with early electronic music across the board. The early experiments in Europe were also relegated to novelty or used for film and television. Early electronic pieces by Varèse in the 1930s and Stockhausen in the 1950s were widely overlooked at the time and for the public in the 1960s anything that sounded demonstrably electronic was still an oddity, used to score sci-fi films, make sound effects or curio synthesiser records. The radical experiments coming out of electronic studios like the GRM (Groupe de Recherches Musicales) in Paris, the studio for electronic music of WDR (Westdeutscher Rundfunk) in Cologne and the Radiophonic Workshop in BBC Maida Vale were funded by public broadcasters and so the music they composed was put to use in film and TV. The sound studio at the NID, while not at that scale, had largely the same role and was often in service to the film or animation department. "At the beginning it was a very alien kind of sound", former student Deepankar explained. "It could be very jarring! I mean we were not in music school, so none of us were going to actually become musicians, so the sound studio was really for making soundtracks for the animation films that were already being made." Despite the progressive ideas of the school, once David Tudor left there wasn't the institutional structure to help contextualise these sorts of musical experiments.

The Moog also arrived at an auspicious moment for the institution. In 1970, a year after its installation, the NID found itself in a quandary. The Ford Foundation, which had been funding it since it was founded, decided to pull out its financial support. Despite it nominally being a national institution, up until then the NID had managed to operate with relative independence from the government but after this point state scrutiny started to intensify. The Sarabhais brought in a retired admiral to help run things and take the pressure off but relations soon turned sour and, after a government inquiry in 1973, the Sarabhais stepped down from their management position. This marked the end of a period of utopian experimentation under their leadership.

Interestingly for our story, in the archives of E.A.T., the engineer and organisation's founder Billy Klüver suggests that it was the arrival of the instrument that broke the camel's back for the Ford Foundation. It was seen as the final piece of frivolity that pushed them over the edge. So in that sense, the Moog is both a symbolic piece of equipment as well as sonic, in that it occupies this hinge in the history of the institute. The instrument became emblematic of a period in the institution's history that it was trying to forget. Once Tudor left there were only a few people who were interested enough to experiment on it and eventually its use became more restricted through fears it might be damaged and it fell into disrepair.

On the last leg of our BBC recording trip we spoke to Alexander Keefe, a journalist who had written an excellent piece on the Moog for the online periodical "East of Borneo".[2] He helped to contextualise the story within the wider history of the nation at that time: "The late 1960s was a moment of reflection for the nation as a whole. Until then India was experimenting with things like the establishment of the NID and new ways of forming national identity. But by the late 60s, there's a cynicism setting in around some of these dreams. Big questions were emerging.

What is design good for in a country like India, in a time like 1969? What is the Moog for and what can it do for India in 1969? The question of utility is very important to the planners of post-independence India, things like the Moog should be put to the service of the nation, as silly as that question sounds, it was actually paramount to their thinking. And if the answer ends up being nothing much, that's part of the problem."

History is built around noise and silence. It's easy to rewrite the story of the electronic sound studio in retrospect, to say that these sound studios were forward thinking spaces of experimentation enthralled to this new musical form, but in reality many of them were also at the whim of their funders and fell out of favour once fashion moved on. Keefe made an interesting analogy: "David Tudor, in his role as a performer of John Cage's music, especially the *Music of Changes*, has to train himself to perform in a disjunctive way on the piano. Tudor has turned himself into a master of ignoring the previous moment and riding these moments of great disjunction, rather than creating the sort of false continuities that would characterise most Western art music. In that way the history of the NID can be seen in a Tudor-esque light as a series of radically disjunctive moments that can only be forced into a kind of melody".

Notes

1   *Electronic India* (2020). BBC Radio 3, 17 May. Available at: https://www.bbc.co.uk/programmes/m000j969

2   Keefe, A. (2013) *Subcontinental Synth: David Tudor and the First Moog in India.* Available at: https://eastofborneo.org/articles/subcontinental-synth-david-tudor-and-the-first-moog-in-india/.

EXPLORING NEW FRONTIERS
AS A STUDENT OF DAVID TUDOR
Jinraj Joshipura

Can the synthesiser help us to decipher animal languages, or develop a new underwater language for submersible vehicles? Can we use biofeedback as a sound source for creating music?

Questions like these were asked regularly by my teacher, the American composer David Tudor, as we explored the new frontiers of electronic music at the National Institute of Design (NID) in Ahmedabad.

In 1969, I was a student of architecture at the Center for Environment Planning and Technology (CEPT). I heard that an American composer associated with the Institute of Experiments in Art & Technology (E.A.T.), who had worked with both the Beatles and John Cage, was coming to teach electronic music at NID. I jumped with joy and cycled over to meet him and learn more. I was just 19 years old. Our encounter was thrilling for me and, I believe, amusing for him.

"Are you a musician and do you play an instrument?" he asked.

"No," I said, "but I am a great listener. I just love music and consider it mankind's greatest original creation. I want to begin studying music: so why not learn something entirely new, rather than relearn what others have mastered for centuries?".

David liked my answers and showed me around. I was aghast to see the sound studio kitted out with futuristic equipment that I had only seen in movies. He played me a few different types of music and asked for my

← Voice recording at the NID sound studio, circa 1970.

analysis and opinions, after which he accepted me as a student—I couldn't believe it! I returned to CEPT and asked permission from its director, B.V.Doshi, and my teachers H.C.Patel and M.C.Gajjar. Professors Christopher Benninger and K.B.Jain also supported my request and I received permission to study at NID.

Our training began with an introduction to the team that Tudor and Gita Sarabhai had brought together from various backgrounds: Sarabhai and Atul Desai (a very accomplished musician), I.S.Mathur (a filmmaker), S.C.Sharma (a sound engineer and poet) and myself, an architecture student. Two other students left within a few days.

The learning process began with an overview of what the Moog synthesiser was, and an introduction to its different components and modules, followed by the other equipment that David had set up in our studio. This included a Bode Frequency Shifter (Model 6552, #1003) a Dual Ring Modulator (Model 6402), two Ampex AG-350-2 2-channel tape machines, a Quad stereo preamplifier and two separate Quad power amplifiers, Tannoy monitor loudspeakers, a Moog mixer with line and microphone inputs, and at least three Sennheiser MD 421 dynamic microphones. There were also tone generators that produced sine, square, sawtooth and pulse waves. To the best of my knowledge this equipment was all funded by the Ford Foundation.

David was an intelligent, innovative teacher who introduced us to a new world of sound synthesis. He showed us that while the synthesiser has all the tools to compose music, it can also generate sounds that are unique.

David was also caring and provided each of us with individual coaching, encouraging us to innovate. The main help that we all needed was learning to use the different components to generate and manipulate sound patterns, and then record them. He worked out a schedule for each student to explore, experiment and compose whatever they wished. He was keen to understand how each of us reacted to the synthesiser.

The other four students worked during the day, but because I was also studying at CEPT, I had to use the studio in the evenings and at weekends. David would stay in late to teach me and guide me; this was

→ Jinraj Joshipura
→ David Tudor with John Cage, Gita Sarabhai

a great sacrifice and kindness on his part as he was staying at the Villa Manorama, owned by the Sarabhai family, at the other end of town. These evenings and weekend interactions gave me more time and opportunities to interact with him.

At this stage of the learning process, I'd diverged from the other students, who were professionals in their fields and at least 15-20 years older than me. Some of them were trying to use the synthesiser to create sounds closer to either Indian or Western instruments and music. My divergence was due both to the fact that I had no musical background and also that I was reading books on sound engineering, music theory and electronics.

After a week I began to perceive the synthesiser as a laboratory for sound and sound waves. I compared it to physics and chemistry labs, where scientists break down materials into compounds, molecules and elements. I thought that the electronic synthesiser and other ancillary instruments made it possible to dissect, decompose and recompose new sounds and so gain access to the full spectrum of audible (approximately 20Hz to 20000Hz for most humans) and inaudible sounds.

My understanding of the synthesiser, coupled with my lack of musical baggage set me on a new trajectory. David listened patiently to my ideas, smiling with amusement. "You are on the right path," he said. "I always wanted someone to experiment with a new approach. So how will you use your new understanding to compose something? Can you devise a conceptual theme and follow it through?"

His comments set me on fire.

Inspired by the space scenes in *Dr. No* (1962), *You Only Live Twice* (1967) and *2001: A Space Odyssey* (1968), I decided to compose music as if I were about to undertake a journey on a space liner in 2001, 32 years into the future. Each of those films featured beautiful background scores, but I thought "If I'm in a space liner, will there be an orchestra on board playing 'Blue Danube'?"

The answer was a resounding no.

I wanted to challenge the very premise of a space soundtrack. My logic was that in space there is no medium through which sound can travel. Hence, in space, one cannot hear the musical accompaniment to Kubrick's film.

So, what would one hear outside the space liner? I believed that only the synthesiser could produce such a soundscape,

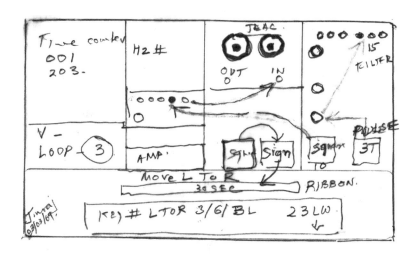

Synthesiser "sheet music" by Jinraj Joshipura, 1969.

Live concert sketch, 1972.

Inflatable interactive sound tunnel at NID, circa 1969.

made up of novel sounds unheard until now. My composition would be a work of pure imagination.

I titled my composition 'Space Liner 2001' and used architectural thinking to conceptualise a journey in which I was sitting in a space liner, watching deep space outside through a domed glass window, imagining what the soundscape out there might be.

I read about how film scores were composed, how a director and a composer would discuss a film's themes during production, listen to musical examples and talk about the direction envisioned for their soundtrack. Sometimes they would view completed shots and scenes to give the composer a feel for the pacing. Then, once the final edit was available for viewing, the complete score would be recorded in a studio, synced to the film, allowing the composer to see whether everything worked.

I used similar techniques, looking at images in books of Earth from space, outer orbits, galaxies, falling stars and nebulae. What I created was a soundscape, like a landscape in the physical world: my musical arrangements were also architected—recorded and documented in drawings so that I could recreate them later.

While preparing my first arrangement I was forced to improvise what I think was the first sheet music for synthesisers. The problem was that, after I had spent a night creating patches, plugging cables into the Moog's various modules, the following day the other students would dismantle them to develop their own sounds. So I needed a way to be able to recreate these patches again, precisely, the following evening.

I expressed my frustration with the situation to David and he asked me how I would solve the problem, which would, after all, occur every day. I told him that I would create a map of my arrangements. And so the architect in me set out to draw the synthesiser with all its knobs, switches and buttons: I used lines to represent cables and arrows to represent inputs and outputs. I made a ledger using numbers to detail frequencies and potentiometer positions for filters and other components. I also added photographs of oscilloscope patterns to show, visually, what the sounds looked like. Little did I know that I had created the first synthesiser sheet music, as shown in the next sketch. David was amused by my innovation and placed the sketch on display. To me, encouraging innovation like this is the hallmark of a good teacher.

My initial piece was made of ethereal sounds, heartbeats and engine sounds constructed using white noise and tone generators—sawtooth, pulse, sine and square waves—as sources. Next I shaped and manipulated these sounds using classic synth modules like oscillators, amplifiers, envelope generators, sequential filters, white noise generators, ring modulators, faders, triggers and mixers, all controlled with a CV (voltage control) keyboard and ribbon controller.

To the best of my memory, my soundtrack began with a loud explosion followed by white noise representing the lift and vertical movement of a space liner, with continuous thrusts modulated by a pulse generator. I also used fades to represent the space liner entering the tranquility of outer space, interspersing silence with random keyboard sounds. The transits of shooting stars were also created using the ribbon controller and faders.

While the students worked, David was preparing a master soundtrack during the nights and weekends, or early in the morning. He had given us a deadline to submit our compositions to tape. However, we didn't know that he was planning a big event, a sound and light show which he described as "incidental music". Later we had learned that the soundtrack to the event was composed of David's work, and our own, mixed and arranged by him.

Different departments of NID were encouraged to join us in creating the backdrop for this audiovisual extravaganza. I worked with a filmmaker and product designer, Arnold Walters from Belgium, to build a carpeted plastic tunnel which featured pressure pads connected to speakers that triggered music as people walked over them.[1]

Later, Manorama Sarabhai arranged a farewell dinner at her home for David. There I got to meet dignitaries including Dr. Vikram Sarabhai, Gautam and Gira Sarabhai, alongside B.V. Doshi and Prof. Christopher Benninger of CEPT.

Prior to this I was invited to lunch with David at the Sarabhais' home to discuss my future plans. I presented two ideas to him: deciphering the language of animals and creating a new communications language for underwater submersible vehicles which could be heard and seen on oscilloscopes. I detailed these in handwritten letters, leading to an invitation from The Rockefeller Music Research Center in San Diego to work on biofeedback.[2]

I couldn't accept their invitation, however: my parents insisted that I finish my architecture course at CEPT, so ending my sonic career. But my education in electronic music gave birth to many ideas, such as the giant synthesiser on a stage I devised for my final year architecture studio (see sketch opposite).

My inspiring, futuristic, and exploratory electronic music education under David Tudor gave me the impetus to explore new subjects like energy, cybernetics, and quantum physics, which lead to my CEPT thesis *CYBERCOLIBRIUM: The Architecture of the Future as a System Open to Information & Energy.*

→ Sketch of stage design by Jinraj Joshipura, 1972.

ARCOLOGY - UNITS — STEEL ARCHITECTURE

SPACE FRAME

SOLAR PV

LIGHT

MECHANICAL ENGINEERING STUDENTS FABRICATING SPACEFRAME IN THEIR SCHOOL.

PREPARE SERVICES
1) ELECTRICITY
2) PLUMBING } BY POLYTECHNIC STUDENTS

STEPS

STEPS

POOL

(8)

(7)

COMMUNICATION ANTENNA

CONTROL CENTRE SCULPTURE

SPACE FRAME

POOL

STREET

SPACE FRAME

STAGE

POOL

1) NATIONAL INSTITUTE OF DESIGN
2) CIVIL / FINE ARTS SCHOOL

DESIGN SPACEFRAME
MECHANICAL / CIVIL / ARCHITECTURE

(6)

(8)

From CEPT I would go on to become a multidisciplinary professional whose work, both pragmatic and hypothetical, has bridged 17 disciplines, several generations, multiple continents and institutions including MIT, the University of Tokyo, The World Bank, IBM, and Dell.

. To this day I attribute my unusual career path to David Tudor's inspiration: he encouraged me to explore new ideas and gave me the confidence to accept challenges beyond my formal education and training.

Over the past few years Paul Purgas, Alannah Chance and Jude Rogers have breathed new life into my dormant musical career and I have again begun to explore the sonic world. Inspired by them, I plan to compose and play music on a contemporary synthesiser, discovering new sounds as a basis for both music and other ideas beyond.

Although I am now 71 years old, I remain an avid traveller and tennis player and am still full of energy. I'm confident that my forward-thinking mindset and positive attitude will enable me to pursue these new musical plans: for the body may age, but the mind need not.

Notes

1 NID must have photos and a film made by I.S.Mathur of this "Incidental Music" show.
2 These have been archived at The Paul Getty Museum in California.

Gita Sarabhai: A Partial Portrait
Rahila Haque

In 1969 Gita Sarabhai made two recordings on the new Moog modular
synthesizer that had arrived at the National Institute of Design (NID)
in Ahmedabad under the instruction of musician and composer
David Tudor. Gita was the sister of industrialist Gautam Sarabhai
and architect Gira Sarabhai, who led on the establishment of the NID
in 1961. A modern Indian merchant family who were supporters of
Mohandas K. (Mahatma) Gandhi and Jawaharlal Nehru, the Sarabhais
were dedicated to a liberal and democratic vision for an independent
India. Their lives were defined by a privilege and exceptionalism that
gave them the resources to build a distinctive legacy across industry,
science, architecture and arts patronage. Gita, Gautam and Gira took a
particular interest in Western avant-gardist cultural practices, bringing
a moment of radical social, political and technological change in India
into dialogue with Western Modernism. Alongside her siblings, Gita
was involved in envisioning the curriculum for the NID and establishing
Ahmedabad as a centre for experimental art and design.

Education, Nationalism and the Hindustani Classical Tradition

Gita's training as a musician was in the Hindustani (North Indian)
classical tradition. Born in 1922 in Ahmedabad, Gita was one of eight
children of the wealthy industrialist Ambalal Sarabhai and Saraladevi

← Portrait of Gita Sarabhai taken in 1951.

Sarabhai. The siblings were raised in a unique home schooling environment devised by Saraladevi, who was greatly influenced by the teachings of Italian educator Maria Montessori and her child-led method of learning, and Bengali polymath Rabindranath Tagore's philosophy of education and pedagogical practice pioneered at Shantiniketan, a visionary eco-conscious school he founded in 1901. Tagore himself incorporated Montessori methods into his idea of an interconnected humanist and naturalist approach to learning, with freedom of expression at its core. These practices inspired Saraladevi to bring in specialist teachers from Cambridge and Shantiniketan, giving her children the opportunity to pursue their individual interests and encouraging a high level of proficiency in their chosen subjects[1]. Gita's exceptional education allowed her to follow her passion for music and she studied for a degree in Hindustani classical vocals at the prestigious Marris College of Music (now Bhatkhande Sanskriti Vishwavidyalaya) in Lucknow. Gita was also one of the first Indian women to play the pakhavaj, a barrel shaped two-sided drum traditionally played by men. Altogether she spent eight "absorbing and rewarding years" studying singing, drums and music theory[2].

I want to consider the environment that Gita was learning in to understand her later thinking, particularly as this period of the late 1930s and early 1940s was one that followed a few decades of major debate and reform within Hindustani classical music. Since the turn of the twentieth century, there had been a drive to remove the traditional system of patronage and hereditary learning that had been led by Muslim ustads. The reality of this saw a struggle to formalise music within the cultural agenda of a growing Hindu nationalist sentiment on one hand (the fascist Rashtriya Swayamsevak Sangh, or RSS, was founded in 1925), and an assimilated colonial influence on the other (the British had been in India since 1757). These reforms led to Hindustani music being gradually dominated by a Hindu majority, despite having evolved through significant Persian Muslim influences since the twelfth century, and being led by Muslim practitioners since Mughal rule in the seventeenth century.

The desire for reform was perpetuated "by elitists, mostly Hindu Brahmin and English-educated reformers...the immediate consequence of the rapid social and intellectual transformations that Indians

Jiddu Krishnamurti in Vienna, 1923. →

T.445   **TDK TAPE 150**

REEL NO. I.   TITLE   SPEED 7.5 i.p.s.

Gehta Khaya.   Mono. single track.

"Frequencies in square and sine wave.
of chromatic scale" (Indian).
Raw material.
Ref. Geeta Mayor.
Recorded on - 1969.
Recorded by - S. C. Sharma.

TIME CHART	Tape Speed		
	19cm/s (7½ips)	9.5cm/s (3¾ips)	4.75cm/s (1⅞ips)
Single Track	30 min.	60 min.	120 min.
Double Track	60 min.	120 min.	240 min.

TDK ELECTRONICS CO., LTD.
950 Japan.

Tape 445 from the NID archives, produced by Gita Sarabhai.

experienced during the imperial encounter."[3] Together with their interest in independence and modernisation, elitist upper-caste Hindus shifted the tradition of Indian classical music away from what they considered to be an "illiterate" Muslim hereditary practice, towards a more "scientific" approach that followed the formalities of the European classical music tradition. It was ultimately the teaching and institutionalisation of Hindustani music as Hindu religious music, by the reformer Vishnu Digambar Paluskar, that created, according to historian Janaki Bakhle, "the commingling of music and sacrality…not as the expression of individual private faith but as a paradigm of public culture."[4]

While an independent Hindu nationalism was at the core of these reforms, they are also discussed by historian Bob van der Linden as paradoxically being influenced by the colonial imagination and the work of various orientalist thinkers, who had since the late eighteenth century claimed that "Hindu music" had declined in the hands of Muslim rulers since its earlier "golden age"[5]. In this account, then, the Hinduisation of classical music is in part an example of the British divide-and-rule tactic; it also signifies that the meeting of the colonial and Brahminical ideas that sought to expunge Muslims, also meant to ensure that those considered lower-caste and Dalits were excluded from classical music practice, in the same way they were (and still are) discriminated against throughout public life. By following the Vedic scriptures, the elites established classical music as an anti-Muslim and casteist cultural practice to extend "their supremacist ideology within the domain of art and culture."[6] While ustads still garnered much respect for their talents and continued to perform, they were forced to make themselves more secular or palatable to a Hindu audience in order to continue working, and were gradually pushed out of learning and teaching in the modern music institutions, including Marris College[7].

In giving this context I want to bring a sense of the complex and turbulent socio-political backdrop to Gita's story; her highest musical training took place in this nexus of nationalism and growing religious division in the decades leading up to partition in 1947. Yet she seems to have been highly aware of and sensitive to the artistic ramifications of the changes taking place, which would lead her to the conversations and avant-garde practices of her later life; a distinctly different path to the one she was dedicated to with her pandits. The NID itself proposed a radically different kind of engagement with the idea of a modern national institution and had little interest in the regressive and discriminatory attitudes of the kinds represented by certain Hindu reformist music institutions.

It is unlikely that Gita would have accepted or adhered to any anti-Muslim and casteist perspectives she might have encountered during her education. Despite coming from a Shrimal Jain family, her father Ambalal had taken as his surname the first name of his father, Sarabhai Maganlal Shah, because "he did not want to take a family name that could be associated with either caste or community or occupation."[8] Ambalal had also long supported the secular democratic ideals of Gandhi and Nehru; and even though Gita herself was not a political activist, she grew up around radical figures including her father's sister Anasuya Sarabhai—a pioneer of the women's labour movement in India. Anasuya led the Ahmedabad Mill Strike in 1918, during which Gandhi (already closely associated with the family) began his first hunger strike in solidarity with the workers, many of whom were Dalits. Although it is important to add that Gandhi was criticised by many throughout his life, including the politician, social reformer and caste abolitionist B.R.Ambedkar, for not fully renouncing the varna system (the division of society based on an individual's characteristics and occupation) as a template for social order, despite his apparent support for the abolition of "untouchability"[9]. Nothing suggests that the Sarabhai family supported the varna system and, undoubtedly, Anasuya's liberalism when it came to equal rights for women was shared by her brother Ambalal, who supported the women around him to be independent and excel in their fields[10]. Gita's eldest sibling Mridula was politicised at a young age and was also influenced by Gandhi, joining the Salt Satyagraha in 1930. She was later appointed to the All India Congress Committee in Gujarat where she focussed on women's rights and became close to Nehru. During the violence of partition she took on active peacekeeping roles as part of her life-long work on Hindu-Muslim amity, before eventually abandoning Congress to support Sheikh Abdullah and Kashmiri independence[11]. Gita was, then, surrounded by individuals that became leading feminist and nationalist figures in India, and defied such regressive cultural ideas that underpinned the work of Hindu music reformists.

Beyond her formal education and practice, Gita's passion for music grew through collecting—she was a musicologist as much as she was a musician—and she amassed a large archive of tape recordings of classical and folk music from her travels around India, giving her a broad appreciation for music that went beyond her schooling. In 1949, Gita established Sangeet Kendra ("music centre") as a way to preserve and disseminate aural tradition, organising baithaks (sessions) and lecture demonstrations and later releasing music by seminal artists (including Muslims) such as Siddheshwari Devi, Surashree Kesarbai Kerkar, Nazakat and Salamat Ali Khan and Zia Mohiuddin Dagar. Despite this passion and dedication, Gita was seemingly uninterested in producing her own music to distribute or to perform publicly. She had a more private and intimate practice that existed in the time she spent learning with her teachers (her status gave her access to many established musicians), having conversations and later, working on very occasional collaborations. Without the need to make a living from her practice, she could be content with listening, sharing and experimenting rather than being centre stage.

In Search of the Occidental: Five Months in New York

Those nurturing early years enabled Gita to maintain a self-directed study of music, eventually leading her to travel to New York in 1946 to learn about Western composition, at the age of twenty-five. At the

David Tudor and Gita Sarabhai in Ahmedabad 1969.

time she already had a deep interest in philosophy and in particular the work of Jiddu Krishnamurti, whose teaching centred around the idea that "truth is a pathless land…limitless, unconditioned, unapproachable by any path whatsoever"[12]. Krishnamurti advocated for a model of freedom without direction; I wonder if this is one of the reasons Gita committed herself to a music practice led by curiosity rather than a focus on performance and attainment. During her trip to the USA, she also attended one of Krishnamurti's camps in Philadelphia and his ideas would remain important for her throughout her life[13].

Gautam made the arrangements for Gita and also for Gira (who was to go and study at Frank Lloyd Wright's School of Architecture at Taliesin) to spend several months in New York. Gautam had recently visited the city and put Gita in touch with his new friend, the sculptor Isamu Noguchi. Noguchi suggested Gita should learn from musicians rather than pursue formal study at Juilliard as she had intended, and he quickly introduced her to the composer John Cage. From her first meeting with Cage, Gita recalled a brief but generous encounter during which he agreed to teach her what he had learnt from Schoenberg at no cost, if in return she would teach him what she could about Indian music[14]. On the five month exchange that followed, during which the

79

two musicians met multiple times a week, Gita's immense influence on Cage has been well documented. It was the beginning of Cage's enquiry into Eastern philosophy and musical traditions that became so integral to the development of his later work in the 1950s and 60s. During her visit Gita gave Cage a copy of *The Gospel of Sri Ramakrishna* by Mahendranath Gupta, an English translation of a classic spiritual text recounting the teachings of the nineteenth century Bengali mystic Ramakrishna—a Hindu Brahmin who integrated the spiritual values of Islam, Christianity and other religions to advocate for devotional life across religious, class and caste lines. The book had a big impact on Cage at a time when his personal and artistic life was in flux[15] and it gives a further indication of the kind of polymorphic figures that Gita herself valued.

According to John Cage biographer David Nicholls, Gita went to New York because she was "Concerned over the ever-increasing threat that Western music posed to the propagation of traditional Indian music", and wanted "better to comprehend and confront this creeping cultural invasion."[16] Elsewhere critic Alexander Keefe, in his work on David Tudor's time in India, has positioned Gita's reasoning as a concern around the effect of "Western musical modernity"[17], a framing that implies she was circumspect about Western experimental music when she would have been unaware of these practices. I think it is important to clarify that Gita's concern was not about avant-garde influences, but rather the encroachment of European classical music forms on Indian music that would have been evident to her from her education at Marris College and the various propositions being made by reformists. In her own recollection of what drove her to New York, Gita explains,

being a purist at heart, I...saw the danger to our traditional music from alien and irreconcilable influences particularly as manifest in harmony developed in Occidental music. The fear was real and stemmed from the high value which was placed on, and the awe with which the new listening public and even some traditional musicians regarded it, without quite realizing its implications on the horizontal and monodic movement of Raga. It, therefore, seemed quite natural to me to acquaint myself with the basic principles of Occidental music in the hope that it would benefit my understanding and readiness to partake of the contemporary situation in India.[18]

It was "the standardization of music theory and practice, notation, music education"[19] under Western influences that seemed to have spurred Gita to want to learn about Western music. Her admission of being "a purist" also suggests that her understanding of a true Indian classical music was already firmly in the realm of form rather than a particular religious, cultural, or nationalist sentiment.

Gita did not fail in her mission; the trip to New York introduced her to many facets of contemporary and historical Western music. Her own accounts are full of detailed descriptions and sharp observations of people and places she encountered during her time in the city. Her studies with Cage included lessons on counterpoint and the twelve-tone technique. In one of her most illuminating statements on the resonances between her and Cage, she said, "even though we came from different musical backgrounds we had basically a similar approach—structural. Moreover, we had the same distaste for harmony and for any extra-musical values and considerations."[20] What Gita had felt in India to be a "danger" to classical music—tonal harmony—found validation through her dialogues with Cage. Cage helped her to understand her concerns and her perspective more fully; she found in his ideas on music parallels to her own tradition, but she could now understand it through the constructive elements of sound, silence and noise.

Gita's time in New York was a life-changing period during which her intensive learning, conversations and outings with Cage were not the only formative elements. Lou Harrison sometimes joined them for dinners and concerts; she had meetings and tutoring with Edgard Varèse (a later influence on the electronic composers at the NID[21]); she learnt the history of occidental music with Curt Sachs; and familiarised herself with operatic traditions through Fritz Lehmann. These interactions all left Gita with a sense of artistic possibility that opened up "new areas of awareness and avenues of perception"[22] beyond her training in Hindustani classical music. The exchanges she had were philosophical as much as they were formal and historical.

In one of his lectures Cage shared that Gita's reasoning for making music was "[to] sober the mind and thus make it susceptible to divine influences."[23] She herself seemed reluctant to place emphasis on divinity (perhaps a distancing from religiosity), instead stating "the real purpose of music is to integrate and centre one's personality or being, to bring it to a state of repose or tranquillity...communication, as understood in the West, is not [music's] true and prime function."[24] Her personal commitment to practice was through the concept of śāntarasa (tranquillity), one of the nine rasa which in Indian aesthetic theory denote nine essences or emotions that might be affected by an artistic work. At her leaving party in New York, she gave a brief performance on the drums which prompted Varèse to tell her that she did not have rhythm and should stop playing. Recalling this moment, she writes, "Though I valued his opinion and was disheartened, I did not think it necessary to give up—after all I was into it more for my pleasure than for performance or achievement."[25]

Sonic Experiments for a New Era

Through her close friendship with Cage, Gita was pivotal to the arrival of electronic music at the NID when the institute was established 15 years after her trip to New York. The interim period between 1946 and 1961 was marked by the immense change and violence of partition in 1947 and the period of nation-building that followed. In the decade after independence, the country was ready to invest in its future and draw international investment to its vision; the Sarabhai siblings established themselves across industries and used their collective knowledge and global connections to create the NID as a distinctive learning environment. Gita set up the sound studio at the NID and amassed a wide-ranging record collection of Indian and Western music that became the soundtrack to the day-to-day activities at the institute. It was she who brought Cage, and through him Merce Cunningham and David Tudor, to the NID and, "Ahmedabad soon became a kind of outpost of the New York downtown scene."[26]

Recent research has brought to light examples of Gita as a playing musician in the 1960s—experimental works made in the ambitious and spirited environment of the NID. Art historian Nancy Adajania's exhibition Counter-Canon, Counter-Culture for the 2019 Serendipity Arts Festival, included a sound composition made by Gita to accompany a nine-screen immersive installation by Dashrath Patel for the India Pavilion at Expo 67 in Montreal.[27] This was possibly Gita's first foray into sound work and it happened two years prior to the arrival of the Moog at the NID. The two recordings Gita made on the Moog in 1969 were her first experiments with electronic sound, recently retrieved and digitised by artist and musician Paul Purgas. Each recording reveals a considered yet playful attempt to engage this strange new technology. In the recording on tape T509, Gita is heard testing the synthesizer's sonic range, producing a suspended drone alongside a series of sound effects and processed vocal distortions. The recording on tape T445, labelled "Frequencies in square and sine wave of chromatic scale (Indian)", makes apparent that Gita was attempting to interpret the Indian chromatic scale using the Moog. The recording is 20 minutes long and features the ascending scales of a saptak (the equivalent of an octave)—a series of seven primary and five auxiliary svaras (notes), making a total of 12 svaras. The recording moves through two versions of saptak using square and sine wave tones. Gita seemed interested in exploring how she could use the Moog as an instrument, bringing familiar structures into her engagement with the possibilities of synthesised sound. During the initial phases of the studio the Moog had a fretless ribbon controller rather than a traditional keyboard, which meant that it could be touch controlled across a continuously variable frequency spectrum, making it more applicable to non-Western scales. In the last seven minutes of Gita's recording, the tonal scales are layered and interspersed with distorted samples of Hindi songs and additional sound effects. This surprising end to the recording introduces musique concrète and sampling techniques that break the structural form of the chromatic scale, creating a montage that utilises the crossovers and distinctions between Indian music and Western electronic sound.

In the same year that Gita recorded her Moog experiments, she also made a soundtrack for *Events In A Cloud Chamber*, one of two experimental films by the artist Akbar Padamsee, known primarily as a modernist painter[28]. Padamsee made the film at the Vision Exchange Workshop (VIEW) in Mumbai, which he founded in 1969 as a space for interdisciplinary experimentation and collaboration. The only print of the film was lost and so far a recording of the soundtrack has not been found, but this work represents another rare instance in which

Gita made sound or music for presentation. The timing and nature of this collaboration makes it entirely possible that the soundtrack was recorded on the Moog at the NID, although she apparently lacked confidence in using the synthesiser. In a 1994 interview, Tudor shared his frustration at working with Gita as she was apparently "like a recluse, very exclusive"[29], going on to describe an occasion he arranged for Gita to present her Moog compositions at the NID when she pulled out at the last minute, afraid that she wasn't good enough. Gita was elusive to Tudor and he didn't understand her reluctance, maybe because he considered performance through the concept of indeterminacy that he shared with Cage, in which aspects of a work are left to chance during its performance. In theory this is not far removed from Gita's own tradition and it is likely that she and Cage shared these ideas too. However, her understanding of improvisation from an Indian classical perspective was one that existed within the learnt rules of the raga and years of practice, something she had not had with the Moog. I wonder whether the occasion was too demanding and she was unwilling to be judged on her performance; understandable given her experience with Varèse in New York and undoubtedly other such encounters with men in music. However, knowing Gita's view of music as a form of repose and a way to centre the self, any insecurity she had was likely also accompanied by an intuitive understanding of whether or not performing at a specific moment would be the right, pleasurable thing to do.

Gita has been something of a peripheral figure in the story of both the NID and the transnational exchanges that characterised the mid-twentieth century avant-garde; this partial portrait attempts to start building a picture of her ideas and contributions. I have considered, and sometimes speculated on, how the changes she was living through interacted with her own views and social position as a woman musician. I am interested in aspects of Gita's musical journey—led by a deep curiosity and appetite for learning—which opened up dialogues that reflect not only a personal evolution, but also an alternative perspective on changes in music during the major socio-political shifts of pre- and post-independence India. Gita was a passionate musician but she was many other things besides; her family describe her as having been a private although warm, down-to-earth and sociable figure. This should be the beginning of a deeper consideration of Gita's work and life, including her travels and music collection; and greater insights into her experiments with the Moog and how electronic music technology might have further shifted her perspective on musical form.

Notes

1   Pallavi Mayor, interviewed by Paul Purgas and Alannah Chance, 5 March 2020.

2   Gita Sarabhai, letter to Roy M. Close, 18 March 1983.

3   Bob van der Linden, "Hindu Nationalism and North Indian Music in the Global Age" in Irfan Ahmad and Jie Kang, (eds.), *The Nation Form in the Global Age: Ethnographic Perspectives* (Cham: Palgrave Macmillan, 2022), 101.

4   Janaki Bakhle, *Two Men and Music: Nationalism in the Making of an Indian Classical Tradition* (New York: Oxford University Press, 2005), 178.

5   Bob van der Linden, "Hindu Nationalism and North Indian Music in the Global Age", 104–105.

6   Avdhesh Babaria, "The Casteist Legacy of Indian Classical Music", *The Funambulist*, Issue 38, 2 November 2021. Available at: https://thefunambulist.net/magazine/music-and-the-revolution/the-casteist-legacy-of-indian-classical-music-2.

7   van der Linden, "Hindu Nationalism and North Indian Music in the Global Age", 113.

8   Danish Husain, "Mallika Sarabhai: The arts are an extremely powerful sweet pill to swallow some bitter truths", *National Herald India*, 30 December 2022. Available at: https://www.nationalheraldindia.com/india/the-arts-are-an-extremely-powerful-sweet-pill-to-swallow-some-bitter-truths.

9   See B.R. Ambedkar, *The Annihilation of Caste* (1936; reis., London: Verso, 2014).

10   Mrinalini Sarabhai, *The Voice of the Heart* (Ahmedabad: Darpana, 2009), 96.

11   Aparna Basu, *Mridula Sarabhai: Rebel with a Cause* (Delhi: Oxford University Press, 1996).

12   Jiddu Krishnamurti, "Speech for the dissolution of The Order of the Star in the East", 3 August 1929. Available at: https://www.jkrishnamurti.org/about-dissolution-speech.

13   Mayor, interviewed by Paul Purgas and Alannah Chance, 2020.

14   Sarabhai, in a letter to Roy M. Close, 1983.

15   David Nicholls, *The Cambridge Companion to John Cage* (Cambridge: Cambridge University Press, 2002), 121–122.

16   Ibid., 117.

17   Alexander Keefe, "Subcontinental Synth: David Tudor and the First Moog in India", *east of borneo*, 30 April 2013. Available at: https://eastofborneo.org/articles/subcontinental-synth-david-tudor-and-the-first-moog-in-india/.

18   Sarabhai, in a letter to Roy M. Close, 1983.

19   van der Linden, "Hindu Nationalism and North Indian Music in the Global Age", 106.

20   Sarabhai, in a letter to Roy M. Close, 1983.

21   "Radio talk about Electronic Music" broadcast on All India Radio, Tape T497, National Institute of Design Archives.

22   Sarabhai, in a letter to Roy M. Close, 1983.

23   John Cage. "45" for a Speaker', *Silence: Lectures and Writing* (Middletown: Wesleyan University Press, 1961/2011), 158.

24   Sarabhai, in a letter to Roy M. Close, 1983.

25   Ibid.

26   Keefe, "Subcontinental Synth: David Tudor and the First Moog in India".

27   Nancy Adajania, "SAF Interview Series", *The Art Issue*, 2019. Available at: https://www.theartissue.in/nancyadajania-saf-interview.

28   Nancy Adajania, *Zigzag Afterlives: film experiments from the 1960s and 1970s in India*, film screening programme (London: Camden Art Centre, 2020). Available at: https://camdenartcentre.org/content/uploads/2022/07/ZigZag-Afterlife-Programme-Essay.pdf.

29   David Tudor, interviewed by Matt Rogalsky, 2 November 1994. Available at: http://davidtudor.org/Articles/rogalsky_inter1.html.

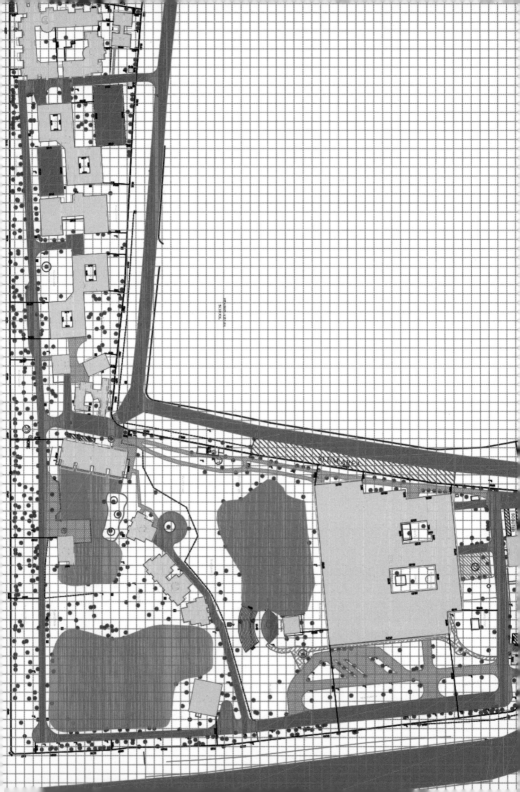

1–6 March 2020, Ahmedabad, Gujarat, India

Matt Williams

The world is not for beholding. It is for hearing; it is not legible, but audible. Our science has always wanted to monitor, measure, abstract and castrate meaning, forgetting that death alone is silent, and that life is full of noise—work noise, human noise, animal noise. Noise bought, sold, or prohibited. Nothing essential happens in the absence of noise...music makes mutations audible, it obliges us to invent categories and new dynamics to regenerate social theory, which today has become crystalised, entrapped, moribund...music is more than an object of study; it is a way of perceiving the world; a tool of understanding...it provides a rough sketch of the society under construction, a society in which the informal is mass-produced and consumed.[1]

This text operates as a travelogue of sorts. It aims to trace the sonic fictions, spatial experiences and complex histories of the various sites navigated across Ahmedabad during a five-day research trip in March 2020. It was my first visit to India, a country that had captured my imagination since my childhood in Coventry. It's a city that indirectly

← Architectural site plan of the NID campus.

draws architectural parallels with Ahmedabad because of its devotion to utopian ideals of modernist design and investment in the wide-reaching redevelopment of civic spaces and supporting infrastructures during the 1950s and 60s.[2]

However, unlike Coventry, Ahmedabad, being the seventh largest city in India with a population of over six million, presented itself upon arrival as an expansive metropolis immersed in a cacophony of sounds—human and non-human—suspended within the ceremonial spectres of its past, wild dogs and sacred cows lingering on street corners. Murmurations of starlings occasionally interrupt the relentless industrial noise accompanying the breakneck speed of logistical and capital expansionism, in part motivated by Prime Minister Narendra Modi's genealogical and political connection to the city.[3]

The trip was consumed with inhabiting and researching the archives, architecture, and landscape of the National Institute of Design (NID). The site of Paul Purgas's aural exploration of India's first electronic music studio. Interrupted only by ambulatory journeys, marked by landmark pieces of modernist architecture, such as Le Corbusier's Sanskar Kendra and Louis Kahn's Indian Institute of Management (IIM). Both sites along with the NID. are material evidence of Western multinational corporations such as Ford Foundation, who operated as a covert channel for the ideological investments of the CIA. in India during the Cold War, and delivered the aesthetic strategies born from the RAND Corporation's influential think tanks.[4] These landmark projects underpinned the ambitions of Jawaharlal Nehru, India's first serving Prime Minister post-independence, to be recognised as a progressive capitalist state and override and suppress the communist dogmas prevalent within Indian society at the time.

On the final day of my visit to Ahmedabad, before flying back to the UK via Air India on a congested flight filled with anxious and nervous passengers apprehensive about the impending pandemic, I visited two distinguished properties associated with the Sarabhai family, who were the founders of the NID. The properties included the Villa de Madame Manorama Sarabhai, designed by the Swiss architect Le Corbusier, built between 1951 and 1955, and the Calico Museum of Textiles, which housed the Sarabhai Foundation. A sprawling complex of buildings from bygone eras filled with material artefacts, beautifully preserved from direct natural light, touch, and thoughtlessness by an arguably overprotective curator, whose incisive knowledge of the collection paralysed its audiences into verbal submission.

Memories of the trip continue to resurface and replay via the various recordings captured navigating the extensive mass of motorways and intersections connecting seemingly incoherent parts of the city. Therefore, this text employs a method of writing that fluctuates between subjective interpretations of the diverse sounds and spatialities recorded when traversing multiple sites during the field study. They sit alongside descriptions of various architectures that give voice to obscured or forgotten narratives—layered like a palimpsest pre- and post-construction.

Pride Plaza Hotel Ahmedabad Judges Bungalow Road Off S.G. Road, Ahmedabad 380054 India to National Institute of Design, Opposite Tagore Hall, Rajnagar Society, Ahmedabad, Gujarat 380007, India

> In history, in social life, nothing is fixed, rigid, or definitive. And nothing ever will be. New truths increase the inheritance of knowledge. New and ever superior needs are created by new living conditions.[5]

Although built shortly after the turn of the millennium in 2003 and renovated in 2009, The Pride Plaza Hotel exemplifies a strand of post-modern architecture that quickly became abundant across the globe during this period. A hodgepodge of construction styles that historian Ina Blom poetically describes in her short essay "Narcotecture" as being a type of architecture "where art deco patterns are allowed to expand to cartoonish proportions, where Muslim geometry fuses with baroque undulation and where the muscularity of pure size informs everything and anything." The Pride Plaza's interior echoes this description and is a type of architecture speculatively built during the rise of finance capital in the early noughties. The building comprises polished marble floors, chrome handrails, and freestanding structures of stained MDF designed to impersonate indigenous woods emboldened with complex patterned fabrics lit by abstract lighting solutions. Upon leaving the

NID campus entrance.

building foyer, guests enter a forecourt outlined by high perimeter walls and an uncompromising security gate, seemingly installed to safeguard the hotel guests from Ahmedabad's constituents. These architectural features create a visually conflicting relationship with the context and heritage of the existing buildings surrounding the development and felt incongruous.

However, despite this seemingly unfavourable critique, the Pride Plaza proved a relaxing and luxurious place to stay during my visit and offered a rare panoramic view of the city. It was the point of departure for my first visit to the NID in an Uber car that zigzagged along partially built and dilapidated thoroughfares. The drive included the Shahibaug underpass, an arterial passage adorned with a freshly restored mural in preparation for a two-day visit of the then-incumbent US President Donald Trump chronicling the various phases of Mahatma Gandhi's life. Trump's visit occurred shortly before my arrival and involved a campaign-style rally with Prime Minister Narendra Modi to illustrate the populist bond between the two men. At the event, Trump boldly declared, "America loves India. America respects India...and America will always be faithful and loyal friends to the Indian people." A sentiment shared by previous US administrations and evidenced by the various institutions they actively sought to facilitate.

The inaugural route to the NID was notable for the collective vehicular sounds emanating from the various motor vehicles filling the roads. A multifaceted acoustic arrangement composed of an assortment of traffic noises that originated from the unrelenting sounds of tires impacting the road surface, accompanied by weary engines, aerodynamic resistance, and screeching brakes. However, the chief contributor to this wall of sound was the continuous honking of horns which would converse in a range of emotions with other vehicles and operated as an automotive substitute for the human voice.

When driving through the city, a recurring topography was the partially constructed expressway planned to project across vast stretches of the city—demarcating areas with priapic concrete structures impaled with metal rods. At night, when returning to the hotel, the erections would be flooded by lithium streetlights and encircled by make-shift shelters that evidenced economic subjugation and the vast proliferation of urban poverty across India.

National Institute of Design, Opposite Tagore Hall, Rajnagar Society, Ahmedabad, Gujarat 380007, India

Sound and space are inherently linked, as sound for us is what disturbs air, and that is not going to happen in the absence of space, but sound also structures space.[6]

The structural, material, and spatial layout of the NID campus felt familiar and adhered to a modernist trope of architectural planning foregrounded by Le Corbusier. A ubiquitous style that quickly became popular within the Western world, duly appropriated by various architects during the Post-War rebuild of Europe and other "developing nations" either directly embroiled in the Second World War or who ostensibly benefited from the seemingly endless influx of economic and cultural investment as a method to ward off oppositional political ideologies.[7]

The numerous blocks built within the grounds of the NID are delineated by luscious coats of grass and tropical vegetation protected from the outside world by rows of trees that outline the site. The purpose-built blocks are constructed from a combination of red brick, concrete pads, and pillars, buttressed by horizontal and vertical steel beams recurringly interrupted by crimson metal window frames filled with a matrix of reinforced glass panels illuminating either a green or jade tint. The building contains interconnecting studios, workshops, laboratories, seminar and lecture rooms, libraries, and offices. Designed to create an environment that encourages and fosters attitudes and behaviour consistent with the fulfilment of the Institute's educational purpose; and to have buildings that are "unmonumental, anonymous, pleasant, unpretentious, workable and unshoddy."—arranged within a grid system that unconsciously choreographs people's movement through the various parts of the campus.[8]

Architectural motifs are repeated across the campus. For example, the polished geometric arrangement of concrete tiles ranging from 50 cm to 200 cm square in size in communal areas was noteworthy and subsequently referenced by Purgas in the various iterations of the exhibition, *We Found Our Own Reality*. These public areas were disconnected from classroom strictures and existed as spaces for collective discussion and experimentation.

The NID felt like an oasis, distinct from its immediate surroundings, which felt chaotic and unregulated. It functioned as a holistic space for learning and knowledge exchange between students and staff, a sensibility, perhaps indebted to its radical pedagogical past, which Purgas identifies as being engendered by a "combination of patrons (Gita Sarabhai), teachers and faculty members (S.C. Sharma, Atul Desai) and students (Jinraj Joshipura)". Together, they established an attitude and an approach designed to create a "platform of group learning" that sought to blur the "boundaries between teachers and students within a practice of collective learning."[9]

At the heart of the NID is the library. A convivial albeit regulated space that provides access to historical information about the situated contexts of the site. Including the previously unheard Moog synthesiser reel-to-reel tape recordings, which Purgas unexpectedly discovered during a visit in 2019. The recordings featured compositions by NID music students between 1969–1972, whom the American avant-garde pianist and experimental composer David Tudor initially schooled. Under his guidance, the students were offered an insight into the synthesiser's technical capabilities and capacity to transform sound electronically.

The discovery of the said recordings has been critical to Purgas's investigation of the NID's electronic music studio, the first of its kind in India. The tapes also triggered an exploration of the political relationship between the United States of America and India shortly after its independence from the British Empire and "evidenced the role of avant-garde sonic practices within an international web of cultural support and soft power." An understanding strengthened by electronic music studio activities, including producing audio compositions for commercial and public use at the Osaka Expo in 1970 at the Indian Pavilion to construct a "modern global identity for India." both nationally and internationally.[10] Additionally, the NID film department used the electronic music studio and the various tape recordings for other projects, which led to the creation of the "radiophonic sound department at NID for future TV broadcasting". Its objective was to bring "decentralised education and learning to poorer rural parts of the country", positioning the studio and the tapes as pivotal tools in the "vision to help bridge the social and cultural divides across the country."[11]

A further motivation for Prime Minister Nehru and his vision for an independent India was to connect disparate regions of India and its peoples, mentally and physically, with the introduction of an indigenous form of Modernism. Although, his ideas were predominantly steered by the West. Particularly the introduction of a transport infrastructure designed to support and accelerate the movement of bodies and commerce decorated by various cultural media, including electronic sound. A relationship that Purgas personally identified with, drawing a connection between Kraftwerk's *Autobahn*, released in 1974, with Jinraj Joshipura's "Space Liner 2001" composition. A correlation that on face value appears tenuous, given that they were produced at different times and continents. However, Purgas explains that "the sense of transit and sound and its cultural interrelation was absolutely within my thoughts" when he was compiling and arranging the materials for the subsequent exhibition *We Found Our Own Reality*. This project included the transposition of the vast amount of audio and visual information unearthed from the NID to create a "narrative transportive movement" that would navigate audiences and enable them to "plot a line across the 30 hours (of recordings) and maintain a sense of dynamism."[12]

The tape recordings of the students' compositions were further anchored to the NID with contemporary field recordings captured by students using a mobile tape recorder to document localised sounds, including the bird song of the starlings who would assemble en masse each evening above and around the trees on the grounds. Alongside these recordings, Purgas made an additional connection with the site by including informal and incidental interactions captured on the tapes. Notably laughter was a frequent expression in the recordings between Tudor and his students. It became a keynote sound for Purgas and was used extensively in the soundwork for his installation through its ability to elicit social and personalised memories of the site. It also connected with a historical performance by Tudor on the campus in 1969, whereby numerous recordings of people laughing were panned across a surround sound PA system positioned at various points across the campus grounds. For Purgas, the altered frequencies of the laughter offered a "cryptic, at times joyful, humorous and eerie" quality with the capacity to evoke "an emotional sense of a place and time at the NID that was sonic yet outside the spectrum of either music or language".[13]

Sanskar Kendra, Bhagtacharya Road, Near Sardar Patel, Ahmedabad, Gujarat 380006, India, and Indian Institute of Management, Vastrapur, Ahmedabad, Gujarat 380015 India

Roads and their margins are ecotones or landscapes of tension where intersecting habitats of plants, animals, cars, bicycles, motorbikes, trucks, trailers, recreational vehicles, pedestrians, beasts of burden and streetcars are ordered by laneways, held and released by traffic signals, covered with dust, gravel, tarmac, and

→ Sanskar Kendra, designed by Le Corbusier.

96

suffused with the whines, roars, thrums, and tickings of passing vehicles, as well as their spectacle, smells, and toxic emissions.[14]

With only two days left, I decided to walk between Sanskar Kendra and the Indian Institute of Management (IIM) in search of an ATM to buy souvenirs from the cash-only shop on campus. With little to no grasp of spoken or written Gujarati, an executive decision to cross the adjacent highway towards a clutch of commercial buildings next to Sanskar Kendra was made. A local museum built before the NID, designed by the architect Le Corbusier, whom Gautam Sarabhai—Chief Architect for the design and delivery of the NID—had assisted when he designed Chandigarh, the capital of the northern Indian states of Punjab and Haryana.

The museum, known locally as the "House of Knowledge", opened in 1956 to accommodate historical artefacts and documents charting Ahmedabad's art, culture, and architectural heritage. It was built as part of a larger cultural centre with separate areas for different subjects such as anthropology, natural history, archaeology, monumental sculptures, and folklores. However, it also existed as the temporary location of the NID during the construction of the existing site between 1964–69.

Sanskar Kendra was constructed using Le Corbusier's signature concrete posts (eleven in total), raised from the ground to lift the building from potential damage caused by flooding while also providing visitors with a shaded respite from the sun. It had the appearance of a bunker elevated from beneath the ground with a limited number of external facing windows presumably incorporated to help with climate control and reduce direct sunlight to preserve artefacts. The choice of materials—red brick, concrete, metal, and glass—was like the physical architecture of the NID, which is understandable given its history and proximity. However, in contrast to the vibrant and dynamic energy of the NID campus, Sanskar Kendra felt redundant and unloved under the supervision of a solitary guard, who sat motionless, seemingly dead to the world, accepting of the silence and monotony of its existence.

In the ongoing search for an ATM, I walk along the busy Netaji and Dr Vikram Sarabhai Marg roads, which leads me to the Indian

Institute of Management (IIM). An impressive architectural edifice protected from the public by large metal gates that provide visual access to see the ambitious proportions of the site. It was built between 1962–1974 following the architectural plans of Louis Kahn in conversation with his staff. A creative process detailed by Kathleen James-Chakraborty in an insightful essay on Kahn's design process and working methods employed during the construction of the IIM, which took place alongside the delivery of the National Assembly in Dhaka. The text opens with an extract from a report written in 1968 by M.G. Siddiqui, a Pakistani civil servant, and Chief Engineer for the National Assembly in Dhaka.

He describes that when he visited Kahn's Architectural office in Philadelphia, US, "Professor Kahn waited for inspiration and then personally supervised further development of his idea at all stages. On most occasions, the original idea and almost each stage of its development are discussed by the Professor with his staff...on many occasions, far-reaching changes are made." Siddiqui's description suggests that Kahn resisted an individualist approach. Instead, advocated a collective process, encouraging employees from different social backgrounds and geographies to share their opinions, ideas, and expertise. An attitude that echoes Charles and Ray Eames's conclusions in the *India Report* which urges a cross-pollination of ideas and practices between the Western modernist values and traditional South Asian craftmanship.

Another prominent figure in the development of IIM was Balkrishna Doshi, a former project architect for Le Corbusier in Ahmedabad and an architecture lecturer at NID. He, along with Gita, Vikram, Gautam, sister-in-law Manorama Sarabhaito and Kasturbhai Lalbhai, invited Kahn to consult on the design and construction of the NID campus and were instrumental in his appointment to design the IIM The involvement of Kahn and Doshi in constructing both sites further illustrates the interconnections between institutions. At the same time, it acknowledges the two-way working process between the Western and South Asian architecture practitioners and the less celebrated figures who facilitated the production of these socio-political and cultural landmarks.

The Calico Museum of Textiles, opp. Underbridge, Jain Colony,
Shahibag, Ahmedabad, Gujarat 380004, India,
and Villa de Madame Manorama Sarabhai
Ahmedabad, Gujarat 380004, India

> Each space, has its own personality that tends to modify,
> position, and move sounds by means of absorptions, reflections,
> attenuations, and other structurally related phenomena.[15]

It is the penultimate day before flying back return to the UK,
and I have organised a trip to the Calico Museum of Textiles. It
was established in 1949 by the Industrialist Gautam Sarabhai
and his sister Gira Sarabhai whose family founded Calico Mills,
one of the earliest textile mills established in Ahmedabad, India,
in 1888. It closed in 1998, with land, plant and machinery sold in
a public auction in the 2010s. The museum was originally housed at
the Calico Mills, which was the heart of the textile industry at the
time. Sadly, it ran into serious financial problems that jeopardised
the funding of the museum's activities, which meant that as the
collection grew, it needed to be relocated to the Sarabhai house in
Shahibaug, Ahmedabad.

The museum was split across two historical sites built at visibly
different periods. The Calico Museum was more expansive, constructed
primarily from indigenous hardwood and dimly lit for conservation
purposes. It featured elaborate displays of different weaving and
printing techniques from the late nineteenth century through to the
late twentieth century. They were presented alongside technically
remarkable Maharashtrian Sarees and shawls, puppets, and embroidery
examples in various styles, including Rabari & Ahir, Kutchi, Orissa,
Bihari, and Punjabi.

The second area of the museum was the Sarabhai Foundation Haveli
which provided a detailed overview of the technical processes, including
descriptions of what the tools could achieve with specific fabrics. The
experience was deeply informative, offering an insight into the past wealth

→ Villa de Madame Manorama Sarabhai, designed by Le Corbusier.

and heritage of the Sarabhai family while illustrating their colonial history and business relationship with the former British Empire. However, the physical and durational aspects of the production of the textiles by seamstresses working on a sub-contract basis from their homes in cramped conditions had a negative effect on their health and subsequently their income. Additionally, due to increased demand for the intricately stylised weaved fabrics, combined with the length of production, and an inadequate number of skilled workers, the technique of printing on fabrics was introduced for expediency and economic purposes.

The acoustics within both spaces variedly dramatically due to the volume of soft, absorbent fabrics in the museum and the instruction for all guests to remove their footwear by the authoritarian curator of the Calico Museum of Textiles, who instilled a sense of trepidation and the potential for being verbally scolded if voices were raised. In comparison, the hard surfaces of the display cases in the Sarabhai Foundation Haveli and the permission to wear footwear created a different sound and energy, accompanied by a constant buzz and drone of tropical species.

A dirt track separated The Calico Museum of Textiles from the entrance of Villa de Madame Manorama Sarabhai, which is surrounded by established tropical vegetation that forms an elegant green fence around the property to create an unforced sense of privacy. The Sarabhai family commissioned Le Corbusier to design and build the property between 1951–55 while he worked on delivering Chandigarh, which was the first city he designed to house half a million people uprooted after the partition of India in 1947. According to information available at the Le Corbusier Foundation, the villa was positioned to take advantage of the "prevailing winds (in order to be traversed by currents of air), and its façades are furnished with brise-soleil" because he believed "comfort is coolness".[16]

The villa is, for the most part, closed to the public, to my luck a private tour of the grounds and the villa was offered by the grandson of Gita Sarabhai. On accepting the invitation, I entered the ground floor of the building, which was open-plan with an architectural element repeated on each of the four floors. Each level featured a private terrace garden, polished geometric concrete floor tiles interrupted by vertical wooden and glass panels, and a concrete staircase. The second-floor terrace had a polished concrete slide that would, at the time of my viewing, finish in an empty swimming pool. Nevertheless, it was easy to imagine the pleasure and unbridled enjoyment it provided for young and old when the building was occupied. In particular, between the 1970s to the early 80s, when it hosted an artists' residency, During this period it temporarily housed a "who's who" of avant-garde and conceptual art luminaries, including Lynda Benglis, John Cage, Robert Rauschenberg, Frank Stella, and John Baldessari among others. Upon arrival, it was customary for an artist to customise one of the many ceiling fans. However, the residency proved so popular that they had all been altered, shifting the artists' attention to the building's walls. For example, John Baldessari painted a large mural of a mosquito that had bitten him.

The craftsmanship, materials, and combination of colours encountered on each floor allowed for a visually seductive experience, leaving an abiding impression in the memory rather than an abundance of photographic documentation, which was restricted. The top-floor terrace placed the viewer in a precarious position due to a lack of balustrades (clearly, health & safety measures would have been an eyesore for Le Corbusier) at a height that matched the canopies of the neighbouring trees. From this elevated position, I experienced the cooling wind that had informed Le Corbusier's placement of the building. It felt secluded, although, in the background, the sound of the nearby motorway could be heard, which presented a low-frequency hum overlaid with the chirping of insects and the sound of tropical birds singing.

Notes

1   Jacques Attali, extract from chapter 1 (Listening), *Bruits: Essai sur L'economie politique de la musique* (1976); trans. Brian Massumi, *Noise: The Political Economy of Music* (*Theory and History of Literature*. Vol 16) Minneapolis: University of Minnesota, 1985.

2   Coventry was a former industrial centre that, from the late 1930s until the 1970s, experienced sustained economic growth. Subsequently, it became a destination for an expansive diasporic population predominantly from South Asia, West Indies, Poland, and Ireland, presenting a breadth of cultures due to the diverse characteristics of its people.

3   Prime Minister Modi resided in Ahmedabad in the late 1960s after moving from the North West region of Gujarat to allegedly work in the canteen of the Gujarat State Road Transport Corporation, which had presumably provided him with first-hand knowledge of the city's infrastructure and desire to

4   Pamela M. Lee, *Think Tank Aesthetics: Midcentury Modernism, the Cold War, and the Neoliberal Present* (The MIT Press 2020).

5   Antonio Gramsci, *Selections from Cultural Writings*, eds. E David Forgacs and Geoffrey Nowell-Smith, trans. William Boelhower (London: Lawrence and Wishart, 1985).

6   Paul Hegarty, extract from *Noise/Music: A History* (New York and London Continuum, 2007).

7   Pamela M. Lee, *Think Tank Aesthetics: Midcentury Modernism, the Cold War, and the Neoliberal Present* (The MIT Press 2020).

8   NID Documentation 64–69, Ranjan MP

9   Quoted from an interview between Paul Purgas and Matt Williams conducted via email between May and July 2022.

10   Quoted from an interview between Paul Purgas and Matt Williams conducted via email between May and July 2022.

11   Quoted from an interview between Paul Purgas and Matt Williams conducted via email between May and July 2022.

12   Quoted from an interview between Paul Purgas and Matt Williams conducted via email between May and July 2022.

13   Quoted from an interview between Paul Purgas and Matt Williams conducted via email between May and July 2022.

14   A. McCartney, 'Listening to Traffic with Guts and Antennae' in Milena Droumeva and Randolph Jordan (eds.), *Sound, Media, Ecology* (2019).

15   Alvin Lucier, 'Careful listening is more important than making sounds happen: The propagation of sound in space' (c. 1979), in Lucier, *Reflections: Interviews, Scores, Writings* (Cologne: MusikTexte, 1995).

16   http://www.fondationlecorbusier.fr/corbuweb/morpheus.aspx?sysId=13&IrisObjectId=5459&sysLanguage=en-en&itemPos=67&itemCount=78&sysParentName=&sysParentId=64.

Subcontinental Synthesis: Dreams & Lost Futures
Paul Purgas

At the heart of the National Institute of Design's campus in Ahmedabad stands a grand tree. First planted in the 1960s its trunk ascends through an enclosing complex of classrooms and workshops, with an expansive canopy of leaves providing a cooling sanctuary to the inner courtyard of Gautum Gira Sarabhai Square. The architectural plan for the site devised by the siblings Gira and Gautam Sarabhai created a modern progressive layout which placed this symbol of nature at the very centre of its pedagogical design, an anchoring emblem of the harmony of humanity and nature that reiterated the institute's holistic ethos, forefronting it as an ecologically conscious branch of the modernist project. The tree's verdant presence articulates a sculptural focus to the site, with its organic form counterpointing against the encircling ring of concrete and glass, emphasising its fluid outlines against the expansive sky and the grid-like configuration of the surrounding campus. At the base, securing buttress roots protrude outwards into the earth, structural tethers alluding to a much deeper knotted and interconnected matrix beneath.

The story of India's first electronic music studio and the curious circumstances that brought this facility to the NID draws a comparison to this grand tree. On the surface the narrative appears simple, a seemingly straightforward account of a Moog synthesiser arriving with David Tudor in Ahmedabad in 1969 and a brief but ambitious period

← Dome of the Indian Pavilion at the Osaka Expo, 1970.

of production that followed. However as the details are observed more closely and the enquiry delves deeper, the more complex this simple story becomes. What presents as easily legible is revealed beneath to be built on an elaborate entanglement of political forces and ideological networks that spreads outwards into far wider systems of culture, power and influence.

The NID sound studio, documented through its tape archive, is a fascinating link in the timeline of electronic music's global expansion across the twentieth century. Its conditions of origin highlight a unique and singular trajectory, one highly specific to the South Asian context, which encapsulates the aspirations and challenges faced through India's journey towards self-determination. The recordings are encoded with the grand scale and utopian dreams of this era, a nascent techno-imaginary that connected the hopes of the newly decolonised subcontinent with a vision to employ art and technology to shape its own destiny. A masterplan to build a progressive future standing proudly on the foundations of an ancient heritage.

Shantiniketan & the Roots of the NID

Rabindranath meticulously tried to bring out the significance of the ancient culture of India, with a view to fuse tradition with modernity in such a way that a new India could emerge in the future[1]

Samit Das

The origins of the NID's pedagogy emerged through the Sarabhai family's ambitions to create a modern education platform that could draw from the twentieth century ideals of Montesorri and the Bauhaus whilst maintaining a grounding within Indian holistic and spiritual thought. Their approach integrated the "learning by doing" principles of Mahatma Gandhi's ashram located nearby in Ahmedabad on the banks of the Sabarmati River, known for its philosophical notion of "shiksha", a practise manifesting as "training that stimulates the intellectual, physical and spiritual faculties".[2] These methods initiated by Gandhi, which resonated

I.S. Mathur & Atul Desai working in the NID studio, circa 1970.

with the Sarabhais, echoed the earlier pedagogical ethos of the poet and painter Rabindranth Tagore and the path shaped by his eco-conscious university Shantiniketan.

Founded in 1901 against a backdrop of colonial rule, Shantiniketan's paradigm for learning focussed on a respect for the natural world, partnered with an ambition to draw out the innate essence of the Indian spiritual consciousness and a grounding belief "that human fulfilment lay in raising each human activity to the level of art".[3] Tagore's values emerged as a means of reconnecting with an ancestral identity predating the subjugated hegemony imposed by close to a hundred and fifty years of British imperial oppression. He held a deeply spiritual perspective on the relationship between time and learning, considering education and consciousness raising as both an immediate action enacted through localised knowledge sharing, as well as a long-term intervention whose transformative potential and impact might ultimately be measured in the duration of decades or possibly even centuries—a pragmatic and temporal duality that balanced the pedagogical demands of the present with the emancipatory shaping of tomorrow.

At the heart of his vision was the integration of arts and crafts practises within personal development, with a strong emphasis on the potential of music as a tool for both artistry and learning. Shantiniketan went on to create its own idiosyncratic musical form that evolved into the ornamented genre known as Rabindra Sangeet (Tagore Songs) which placed equal emphasis on structure and musicality as well as the poetic and political capacity of song. The holistic and cross-disciplinary thinking explored at Shantiniketan, placed learning in a direct dialogue with sound and music, sitting in a continuum with the founding ideals of the NID studio, where sonic innovation fused with pedagogical freethought and liberated experimentalism. At their heart Shantiniketan and the NID both understood the value that music and culture possessed in shaping transformative realities and the vital importance of the sonic in building new futures.

Independence & the World Stage

No mechanism or medium exists...for putting Indians and Americans into mutual cultural contact. The result has been a real void in all efforts toward mutual understanding. This void, serious in itself, is rapidly being filled by USSR and China, as well as the satellite nations. These countries are sharply intensifying their cultural activities and support of "cultural societies" in India and our information is that these are making a deep impression.[4]

Douglas Ensminger | Ford Foundation

The years post-independence created a monumental remapping of the geo-political stage across South Asia, and following 1947 as the British retreated after almost two centuries of colonial dominance, the resulting power vacuum became glaringly apparent. Despite India's first prime minister Jawaharlal Nehru's public addresses in the years preceding independence that proclaimed the nation's intent for a non-aligned position between the global superpowers, the United States was still deeply anxious about what the region's new social and political consciousness entailed. Consequently a strategic decision was made to branch out from funding agricultural and social development projects in South Asia, and more proactively seeking out cultural opportunities and industrial partnerships. Key agents of this policy emerged as the residency and cultural programmes of the J.D. Rockefeller III Fund and the investment work of the Ford Foundation, both of which delivered the governmentally requested conditions for more direct contact between Indians and Americans.

As the Cold War developed across the 1950s the mechanics of the "state-private network" became gradually repurposed by intelligence agencies as a covert vehicle for promoting Western ideological imperialism in order to overthrow and suppress socialist expansion within developing nations. The relations between state and independent philanthropy ran opaquely deep as private anonymous finance was engineered to do the work that governments could not legitimately be seen to do. This emerged through CIA-backed organisations such as the "Congress for Cultural Freedom" co-opting scholars and artistic networks to platform anti-communist propaganda[5], and philanthropic enterprises like the Ford Foundation that channelled funding and policy influence through colonial nations and non-aligned regions, such as India, under the auspices of foreign development aid.[6] America's agenda accelerated after the Bandung Conference hosted in West Java in 1955, as the global axis tilted when representatives from twenty-nine governments of Asian and African nations gathered to discuss peace and the role of the Third World in relation to the Cold War, economic development, and decolonization. The conference was led by India's leader Jawaharlal Nehru, with his energising message for countries to dispel the nostalgic impulse to revert to pre-colonial times but instead look towards present opportunities and new futures.

At the height of these turbulent events the Museum of Modern Art in New York entered the frame of cultural agents operating in South Asia, offering a legitimising institutional facade to covertly address growing US governmental fears. Fulfilling the remit for mutual cultural contact between India and America became one of the key aspects of the 1955 exhibition "Textiles and Ornamental Arts in India" hosted at MoMA in New York as a large scale survey of Indian crafts and fabrics accompanied by a music, dance, and film programme which included the master sarod player, Ali Akbar Khan, and the legendary Bharatnatyam dancer Shanta Rao.[7] It took place at a particularly charged moment when Nehru had not only adopted a commanding role at Bandung but had also received a warm welcome during his state visit to the USSR. Within this unstable political climate the MoMA exhibition strategically helped to salvage ailing American influence within Indian networks.

The project was followed closely by the extraordinarily ambitious 1959 MoMA touring exhibition "Design Today in America and Europe". Housed in a giant geodesic dome designed by Buckminster Fuller the exhibition assembled a collection of approximately 300 design objects and furniture items that toured across nine cities in India, featuring everything from Mies van der Rohe 'Barcelona Pavilion' chairs, Alvar Aalto stools and Wilhelm Wagenfeld glass tea sets, to modern Italian sewing machines, slinkys and ice-cream scoops.[8] The exhibition, masquerading as a design survey, covertly operated as an aesthetic trade show, one intended to entice and embed Western capitalism and materialist desires within the Indian middle classes, a costly cultural gambit to flip the nation towards an American modelled consumer society.

Committed US investment in direct meetings and cross-cultural encounters between America and India created many of the seeds for the emergence of the NID. Charles & Ray Eames's involvement with MoMA's 1955 textiles exhibition introduced them to Indian officials who with Nehru's backing commissioned the Eameses to devise a prospective evaluation report exploring how design education could be established within a newly independent India. This enquiry manifested as the 1958 document *The India Report* which became the foundational blueprint for the National Institute of Design. Likewise with the Sarabhais' support and partnership finance from the Ford Foundation many figures from the international avant-garde came to Ahmedabad during this period including Louis Kahn, Alexander Calder, Jean Erdman, Iannis Xenakis and Le Corbusier who went on to design multiple villas and municipal buildings across the city. However it was perhaps a later one of these face-to-face encounters that initiated a curious thread of the Moog's story in Ahmedabad. This was the first meeting between another of the Sarabhai siblings Vikram Sarabhai, the older brother of the NID composer Gita, who in 1967 met for the first time the Swedish engineer

Billy Klüver[9], founder of the New York based organisation E.A.T. (Experiments in Art and Technology). This interaction would initiate a dialogue of far-reaching technical ambitions between America and India that bonded the new nation's post-independence development programmes with a radical network of New York avant-garde artists, engineers and thinkers.

E.A.T. & the Sarabhai Connection

He who can listen to the music in the midst of noise can achieve great things[10]

Vikram Sarabhai

As revealed on the NID tapes, despite the electronic music studio not being formally connected to E.A.T. activities in India, David Tudor is listed with the organisation's name in parenthesis on the accompanying notes. It is likely that E.A.T.'s links to Tudor offered a more presentable veneer than the more avant-garde framing of him as a composer, and would have provided a greater legitimacy to bringing such an experimental artist into the circles of the NID along with the Moog's acquisition. Tudor's previous correspondence with Ahmedabad and the Sarabhais dates back to his initial dialogues with Manorama Sarabhai and his first visit to the city in autumn 1962 as well as links to Gita Sarabhai through John Cage. Now expanding on the family's artistic ties to the group, Vikram's meeting with Billy Klüver added a new point to this constellation, forming a much more technologically ambitious facet to the family's engagements with E.A.T.

Vikram, a respected physicist and astronomer, was at this time on the cusp of setting up ISRO (the Indian Space Research Organisation), the nation's equivalent to NASA. This followed on from his successful founding of the Physical Research Laboratory in 1947 which conducted extensive investigations into cosmic rays around the same period his sister Gita was studying in New York with Cage. Amongst Vikram's dreams for a new India was the possibility of rapidly educating the country's poorest and most deprived rural communities. He believed the solution lay in developing a new infrastructure for knowledge and learning by employing satellite television as a powerful educational broadcasting tool, which could instigate a rapid modernisation of rural areas through teachings on literacy, healthcare and agriculture. Just one year before meeting Klüver, Vikram Sarabhai had presented a proposal to NASA for a collaborative television test experiment in India using one of their ATS satellites, and having tabled his plans for the vital hardware infrastructure from the US he was now looking to problem-solve the issues of software and content for this future TV network.

The Anand Project, an early experiment in video content creation, was realised through a partnership with E.A.T. and Vikram Sarabhai in December 1969, and occurred notably around the same time of David Tudor's visit to the region. The exercise was centred around rural villages in the surrounding state of Gujarat that operated within the Anand Dairy Cooperative, located 50 miles outside of Ahmedabad, and concentrated on information and instructional videos for the workers who raised and tended milk-producing buffalo. The project investigated the use of early video technology to collect material to be made into educational programmes, and formed part of an early problem-solving exercise for Vikram Sarabhai in conceiving a methodology for localised media production.

The activities of E.A.T. around Ahmedabad formed part of the organisation's longer term plans to create a formal "E.A.T. India" division, which was intended to be headed up by the modern dancer Chandralekha, a key figure within the Indian avant-garde. With these grand schemes in mind the National Institute of Design seemed like the perfect context to anchor this new outpost's tentative development. An ambitious programme was put forward for E.A.T.'s involvement at the NID which would establish the New York organisation with a key role within the institute's syllabus but this was rejected by the Sarabhais and subsequently downscaled into a plan for selected E.A.T. members to participate within the academic setting and an additional agreement for E.A.T. to help secure technology from the United States, in particular technical equipment relating to the production of art and music.[11]

The early 1970s saw E.A.T. develop several key projects in India through financing from the J.D. Rockefeller III Foundation, such as the initiative "American Artists in India" taking place from 1970–71 which saw the likes of La Monte Young and Marian Zazeela, Trisha Brown, Terry Riley, Steve Paxton and Yvonne Rainer participate in extended residencies across the country. Alongside this was E.A.T.'s seminal telecommunications project "Q & A", a 1971 commission by Pontus Hultén at the Moderna Museet in Stockholm that linked a network of telex machines, functioning as typewriter interfaces connected on a global telephone exchange to create a pre-internet chat experience. Conversations were conducted through the interconnected telex machines, one installed at the NID in Ahmedabad and linked up in real-time to similar terminals in New York, Tokyo and Stockholm. The framework invited participants to engage in an exchange of questions, enquiries and speculations between these locations and cultures about what life would be like in the future as part of a collective imagining on ecology, politics, societal values and new technologies. Further East at the same time E.A.T. was pioneering its grandest vision yet, the monumental Pepsi Pavilion at the 1970 Osaka Expo, being conceived as the organisation's magnum-opus, and India became a convenient stopping point during their ongoing dialogues with Japan.

Despite the eventual outcome that a formal E.A.T. India division never materialised, this period saw an impressive array of collaborations between the New York organisation and the National Institute of Design. The artistic and technological principles of E.A.T. found a harmonic mirroring in the dreams and expansive ambitions of the Sarabhai family who possessed a profound understanding of the potential for art and experimental media to shape the new India. Likewise for E.A.T., as an organisation built on the convergence of art and industry in a critical moment when the wider political and commercial forces of the West were beginning to harbour a growing scepticism towards the functional benefits of connecting these worlds,[12] the opportunity to expand operations into new global territories offered a valuable lifeline for ensuring its own continued survival. It was a mutually fortuitous meeting of worlds.

Bob Moog and team with the NID synthesizer crated for transit.

Ahmedabad's Moog

> This music must reach the masses and the listeners must be made
> to realise the vast potential of this sound world[13]

Atul Desai

The origins of the sound studio date back to 1964 as the Ford Foundation
provided resources to develop this area of NID's activity through
a gradual accumulation of tape recording and playback technologies.[14]
This informal facility amassed an impressive collection of field
recordings documenting sounds from around the state of Gujarat.
Much of this part of the NID collection still remains undigitised, but
represents a valuable sonic archive in its own right, with numerous
recordings being gathered under the guidance of Gita Sarabhai.
Building on this initial foundation of a sound studio, and supported by
Gira and Gautam's plans to bring cutting edge technology to the NID,

Gita was requested to oversee creating a residency for David Tudor in Ahmedabad to facilitate the installation of the synthesizer as well as several tape machines. The story of the synthesizer's early origins is revealed in a photograph from Moog's archives, showing Bob Moog and his team standing proudly next to a wooden crate outside the factory in Trumansburg, New York, containing Tudor's Moog marked up for transit and about to begin its journey to Bombay.

It is important to consider the cultural context into which the Moog was arriving, illustrated most clearly by the extensive vinyl record archive in the NID library gathered across the period of the 1960s. Developed by Gita Sarabhai and interspersed with many records from her personal collection there are albums by Terry Riley, John Cage and Karlheinz Stockhausen intermixed with a comprehensive selection of Indian classical music including works by Ravi Shankar, compilations of Tagore Songs and multiple recordings by the celebrated Northern Indian vocalist Kesarbai Kerkar, whose interpretation of Raga Bhairavi was later included in the Golden Record sent into space aboard the 1977 Nasa Voyager probe.[15] There are anecdotal accounts that in the early days of the NID, records from the collection would be played out loud at lunchtimes across the campus PA system, an indicator of their considered value within the academic ecosystem and the influence of the sonic within the school's pedagogical consciousness. The records reveal that the Moog, whilst a complex instrument operationally, was not arriving within a vacuum of sonic culture, but instead had the seeds of a context and appreciation that had been incubated to some degree by the Sarabhais. This is reiterated through the only surviving recording of the NID composers, in which Atul Desai and I.S. Mathur talk about their work during a 15-minute interview on All India Radio in 1970. On the programme they play several of their own pieces whilst discussing their individual perspectives on electronic music, espousing their respect for the compositions of Edgard Varèse and John Cage and enthusiastic appreciation for Wendy Carlos's 1968 album *Switched on Bach*.

The electronic music studio's primary operational window revealed through the tape archive is from 1969 to 1972, and demonstrates a diverse array of aesthetic and structural approaches to sound. These include tape collages, soundtracks, electronic improvisations inspired by ancient rhythmic talas, field recordings, spoken word and phonetic experiments, and effects processing of traditional Indian instruments such as the tanpura and tabla. The recordings come to an end towards the autumn of 1972 with S.C. Sharma being the final composer to appear on the tapes. His composition "Dance Music", a collection of three rhythmic proto-techno arrangements, was meticulously assembled through numerous tape edits to realise the final result. The level of craft present on this reel reveals a diligent evolution from single-take improvisations to this later mode of forensically splicing multiple recordings from the Moog to create elaborate compositions. From conversations with alumni of the 1970s it appears some students intermittently gained access to the Moog after the time of Sharma's final tapes but these sessions if they were ever recorded were not archived at the NID as formal productions.

There is a distinct strand of experimentation within the tapes that is focussed on resynthesizing environmental sounds with the Moog, such as running water, rain, wind and animal sounds—an influence that mirrors David Tudor's own artistic interests and his personal recordings with the NID synthesizer. Tudor's energetic tape titled "Birds", which curiously reappeared 10 years later in March 1979 under the title "Monobirds" as part of a performance at the Xenon nightclub in New York,[16] reproduces high pitched bird song through analogue oscillators and rapid cyclical envelopes. This encompassing awareness of sound and the environment that was a pillar of Tudor's practise resonated deeply with the pedagogic culture at the NID, an institute looking to explore art and design within a harmonic dialogue with the natural world.

Towards an Indo-Futurism

The chorus of frogs, crickets and jackals grows in volume, and is joined by a humming sound. In a blaze of light something descends on the pond, shattering its placidity...A dome-like object is seen sinking into the water. The pulsating light that emanates from it dims into total darkness as the object slowly disappears below the surface.[17]

Satyajit Ray | Screenplay for The Alien

The vast dome of India's Pavilion at the 1970 Osaka Expo, was situated not far from E.A.T.'s own grandiose Pepsi Pavilion, and was realised by the architects Jasbir and Rosemary Sachdev, a husband and wife practise with links to Le Corbusier and a reputation for education and municipal design. Overseen by Vikram Sarabhai, the pavilion symbolised a meeting place of the convergent themes of the ancient and modern, its brilliant white surface emblematic of both the monuments of the past and the tabula rasa of the newly emancipated nation. Housing a presentation of Indian craft, culture and technology the interior featured a soundtrack developed by Atul Desai at the NID that integrated compositions from the Moog, and formed the second chapter of the sound studio's relationship with the World's Fair format. Three years prior Gita Sarabhai had overseen the development of the soundtrack for the Indian Pavilion at the Montreal Expo in 1967, a large-scale exhibition conceived as a narrative from the Indus Valley civilisation to the present. Its celebrated entrance depicted an immersive journey through India presented as a 9-screen 360 degree projection devised by the visionary artist and designer Dashrath Patel,[18] and was accompanied by field recordings and music assembled by I.S. Mathur.

The central role of the NID in developing the media and sound for both of these internationally significant events gives a clear testament to the government's belief in the institution as a platform for cultural innovation, locating experimental film, field recording, sound collage and electronic music within these grand futurist gestures. At twenty years post-independence the growing potential for defining the future through media, incorporating new technologies of sound and image making, was beginning to emerge as part of a cultural strategy for high profile presentations, offering a method to fuse the possibilities of science and technology with the lyrical aesthetics of poetry and the arts. As India's techno-imaginary dawned, it had to consider the broader socio-economic conditions it was responding to, and the need for technology to inspire dreams and political momentum whilst creating the necessitated strides towards a functional modernity. The country being primarily centred around agriculture and farming, and experiencing vast poverty, predisposed its particular requirements for cultural and technological development as being notably different from the conditions of most Western nations. Any new reality that India was to cultivate, had to hold the potential to carry tens of millions of people forward with it in order to make a valid success of its post-colonial freedom.

Alongside the progressive dreams of culture, design and industry which evolved post-independence, science-fiction literature was also starting to grow significantly in popularity. The ability for the genre to pre-empt futures and usher in prospective new realities was beginning to chime with India's grand-scale social and technological visions, and a rise in interest across the 1960s led to what would become science fiction's "golden age" within the subcontinent.[19] During this period the region saw its first science-fiction journal *Ashchorjo* (Amazing) developed by Adrish Bardhan in 1963, featuring articles, serialised novellas, film reviews and intriguing facts about the cosmos. 1967 also saw the development of *The Alien*, an unrealised feature film by Satyajit Ray, exploring a spritely and technologically advanced extraterrestrial's arrival within a village in rural Bengal. Jinraj Joshipura's NID composition "Space Liner 2001" arrives in synchrony with this timeline. Produced in the autumn of 1969, it was the 19 year-old designer's first attempt at creating a completely self-generated sound work, and took the form of an imagining of what it would be like to be a traveller aboard an interstellar spacecraft. Joshipura's composition made with the Moog and tape collaging, is one of the notable examples of a piece of intentioned sonic-fiction within the archive, a recording that offers a glimpse of an avant-garde South Asian science-fiction inspired sound world.

The development of space exploration and electronic music emerged as two closely charted and interwoven histories across the twentieth century. As the theremin soundtracked science-fiction films of the 1950s, providing the early archetype of futuristic sonics,[20] the operational bleeps from Sputnik 1 heralded the first sounds audible by humanity from space.[21] Electronic music became framed in the public consciousness as the definitive sound of the cosmos. In the story of Ahmedabad the interconnection between these two spheres took a unique path in the work of the brother and sister Vikram and Gita Sarabhai. With Vikram in 1969 founding India's space programme, at the same moment Gita Sarabhai developed the nation's first electronic music studio—a techno-poetic mirroring that reiterated the Sarabhai family's comprehensive vision to shape the manifold facets of the new nation.

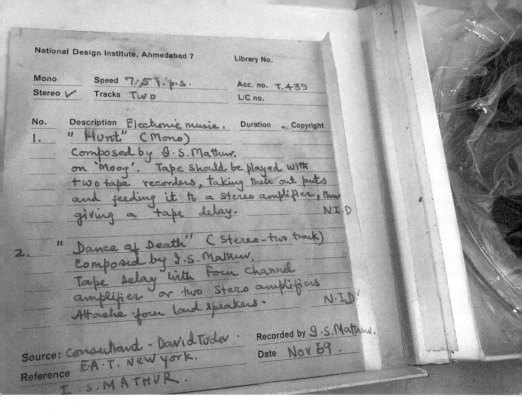

Tape 439 interior reference notes.

The Studio & its Applications

> The change India is undergoing is a change in "kind" not
> a change of degree.[22]

> *Charles & Ray Eames | The India Report*

The NID's studio whilst carrying many hallmarks of an avant-garde
project, having been set up with the oversight of Gita Sarabhai and
subsequently David Tudor, who both held an interest in experimental
sound and composition, the question of its long term application
and use value was inevitably part of the NID's quandary. Being the
defining academic platform at the heart of India's nation building
programme the acquisition of such an expensive Moog modular
system would ultimately have to find some tangible benefits to warrant

such a financial commitment beyond the idealistic pursuit of pure sonic experimentation.

Encircling the moment of the Moog's arrival in 1969 there were the beginnings of a turning point taking hold in growing political tensions between the prime minister Indira Gandhi and Richard Nixon. The increasing uncertainty of long-term financial support from the US forced the Sarabhais to have to open channels of communication with some of the more bureaucratic sectors of the Indian government. These were officials that had a very diminished interest in experimental art for art's sake and were looking for more practical demonstrations of what design and industrial production could do for India. For the NID this process of reorientation marked the beginning of the end of the institute's founding freethinking principles as government intervention looked more closely for clear examples of use value, as well as more prosaic lesson structures and syllabus planning. The pedagogy began to migrate towards familiar and conventional teaching methods rather than the holistic ideals that had previously defined the school, and for the Moog and sound studio the implications of this shifting of priorities left the facility in a vulnerable position.

To complicate matters further the sound studio itself lacked any specific curriculum or academic programme and was framed as an adjunct facility to the more formalised film and animation department, with soundtracks, advertising and radio jingles being some of the commercial outcomes of the studio that provided a more legible application for a modernising India. These activities, supplemented with the more high profile presentations of sound work at the 1970 World's Fair, would have helped counterbalance some of the scrutiny that surrounded the studio's development. Nonetheless the facility was floating in troubled waters as external bureaucrats and even other departments within the NID itself began to critique the expense and reasoning behind an elaborate sound studio inside a design school, and the Moog became a derided symbol of the Sarabhais' opulent misdirection of funds at a time of growing precarity.

Decoding the mystery of what might have been the longer term intentions for the studio potentially lies in further reflection on the ambitions of Vikram Sarabhai and his belief in a satellite broadcasting network for India. Within this web, an initial point to reiterate is the detail that despite Tudor's presence in India not being in any formalised capacity connected to E.A.T., many of the tapes were labelled with E.A.T. after his name in parenthesis. Though small, this annotation highlights the blurriness of the lines occurring between NID and E.A.T. activities during this moment. Likewise Vikram Sarabhai although not formally linked to the NID definitely attended one of David Tudor's electronic workshops with keen interest[23] and was demonstrably in the process of determining his own strategies for media production.

Further to this, following on from Tudor's visit in 1969 and The Anand Project, Lowell Cross, one of the contributing artists for E.A.T.'s Pepsi Pavilion in Osaka, came to the NID for over a month in April 1970 to help fine tune sound equipment in the electronic music studio whilst simultaneously assisting the Sarabhais with the development of a test experiment in Gujarat that was looking to further explore the potential of satellite broadcasting. So it is evident that the two enterprises were being discussed in parallel. The only existing photograph of the NID studio after 1969 shows the Moog installed inside the facility with composers Atul Desai and I.S. Mathur at work—in front of the synthesizer is a keyboard, which had been added later to the system to supplement the original ribbon controller brought by Tudor, and notably to the left of the image installed next to the Moog is now a television set, an indicator that video technology was now entering into a direct dialogue with the studio's work. Together these details build a speculative premise for the NID's sound studio not only existing within the Sarabhai family's creative and academic vision, but also connecting to Vikram's broader requirements for a production facility to soundtrack new programmes for satellite broadcasting.

Previously the common paradigm in the West had been to employ terrestrial ground-based transmission to construct TV networks. This was through TV towers and transmitter masts, beginning in the densely populated cities and gradually moving outwards to access rural and remote areas, a similar principle to how mobile phone networks would be rolled out in later decades. The basis for this approach was a model of moving from the core to the periphery, servicing first the most concentrated areas of the populace and moving outwards to address sparser and more remote communities. Vikram's vision lay in a total inversion of this Western method. Instead he believed the most rural areas to be the places most in need of technological support, requiring education and development through resources addressing literacy, healthcare, agriculture and manufacturing skills. He hoped with the use of satellite television, rather than the cities, these remote and poorest areas of the country could be addressed as the priority and be broadcast to first, with the intention of aiding rapid development in some of India's most deprived communities. It was a techno-utopian programme of visionary scope and ambition.

The stage was now set to realise this through a brokered partnership with NASA, using a geostationary ATS satellite as an anchor for a TV test planned to take place across one year from 1972–1973[24] with NASA using the mutually beneficial situation to field-test the theoretical potential for their own ATS technology to be used for television transmission.[25] It was a win-win for both parties. So it transpired that on the 18th September 1969, roughly one month before David Tudor's arrival in Ahmedabad, Vikram Sarabhai signed his official deal with NASA for the agreed use of their satellite for what he dreamed would be a paradigm shift for the new nation. It is within the context of Vikram's plans that the purpose of the NID sound studio can be read as the first steps in developing a potential Radiophonic type of broadcasting infrastructure in India. A way to realise electronic soundtracks, effects and background music for a future satellite television network that would bring decentralised learning to the masses.

The End of the Dream

He wants us to tilt in favour of Pakistan[26]

Henry Kissinger | The Anderson Papers

The tapes in the NID archive span the years from 1969 to 1972, with the majority of activity occurring in the first two years leading up to January 1971, then a gradual slowing of recordings until September 1972. Deciphering this timeline requires a revisiting of the eroding lines of communication between Delhi and Washington that accompanied this period. By the late 1960s it was felt in US Intelligence circles that India was not responding well to the various development strategies being exercised to bring it in line with Western ideals, and instead was drifting towards Soviet influence. Progressively as tensions rose across the early 1970s American funding through enterprises like the Ford Foundation started a gradual withdrawal from India, driven by shifts in governmental policy that de-prioritised cultural investment programmes. This process reached a dramatic and rupturing climax in December 1971 as Richard Nixon decided to tilt policy and economic support towards Pakistan during the outbreak of the India-Pakistan War in a bid to gain previously unobtainable diplomatic access to Pakistan's ally China, whilst deliberately stoking the embers of the 1962 Sino-Indian War.

His decision triggered a geo-political rupture in the region, and the abrupt end to an era of political and economic support that formed a vital lifeline for Indian art and culture. The impact of these events at the NID became immediately evident as the economic conditions that had enabled its radical experiments within pedagogy and design began to fall away, and anxieties escalated within the institute towards managing and maintaining specialist hardware like the Moog. The response was to start placing equipment under lock and key, restricting access through fears of any damage and costs of repairs. In parallel the dialogue with NASA for using the ATS satellite also ground to a halt, leaving the Moog and sound studio in a doomed position as any implicit long-term strategy for its application in broadcasting slipped away.

It was only several years later in 1975 that relations with America had cooled enough to revisit NASA's involvement in satellite broadcasting plans and an ATS-6 satellite was finally moved over the Indian Ocean.[27] The outcome known as SITE (the Satellite Instructional Television Experiment) distributed television sets to two thousand four hundred rural villages across six states to test the broadcasting of educational programmes in what would become an era-defining moment. Despite the experiment being technically successful, by that time Vikram Sarabhai had passed away and the project had lost its erudite utopian driving force. In addition the political momentum for rural education had become greatly diminished, with satellite broadcasting for provincial development eventually being totally phased out of India's national agenda.

The delay also inevitably meant that the NID sound studio had no direct involvement in SITE, having ceased operations three years earlier. In light of this chain of events the Moog can simply be seen to have arrived at the wrong moment in time, and turbulent political and economic circumstances were destined to extinguish its potential before it had the chance to flourish. Perhaps if events had played differently and American support had remained with India in this crucial window, allowing electronic music's role in a broadcasting network to take hold just a few years earlier, then there may have been a significant expansion of Radiophonic production within India. This alternative path could have activated a much wider interest in exploratory sonic production in the region, making the tapes at the NID the potential beginnings of a much larger history of electronic sound within South Asia.

The Afterlife of the Sound Studio

The story of the NID studio plots out a far-reaching and entangled path. Much like the roots of the institute's great tree, the establishment of the facility reveals a complex set of interconnections and ambitions, a matrix of multiple private and political agendas, and a meeting place of several ideological ecosystems, intersecting at points of support, exchange and extraction. What has been mapped is simply a portion of this system, and many questions remain to be understood in order to fully understand the project of India's first electronic music studio and its impact and afterlife.

The journey of many of the NID composers retained a connection to the worlds of sound and music long after the closing of the studio. Gita Sarabhai spent much of her later life recording concerts of Indian classical music, amassed through an extensive tape archive of her own. Her experimental electronic soundtrack to the 1969 film *Events in a Cloud Chamber* still remains as one of the elusive lost pieces of the puzzle that will hopefully one day be located. Atul Desai and S.C. Sharma remained life-long friends; bonded through their experiences, they continued their own personal explorations within music. Atul Desai kept in contact with David Tudor, and as his Indian classical profile developed he began touring the USA regularly from 1978 and for many years would meet with Tudor on these visits, where they discussed electronic sound and modern music in dance. Desai went on to work extensively with Kathak dance composition and produced a 1982 work titled "Atah Kim", where he mixed electronic elements with the sounds of the sarod,[28] a recording developed in his own studio named Dhwani in Ahmedabad which he setup with S.C. Sharma's support.

I.S. Mathur and Jinraj Joshipura pursued their own academic paths within moving image and design. Mathur went on to instruct classes on animation, film and sound at the NID across a lifelong career within education. Whilst Jinraj Joshipura, the last surviving composer, is now teaching in Puerto Rico, and after 50 years within the worlds of architecture and engineering still feels the powerful pull of electronic sound, and may one day return to synthesisers to continue his own sonic journey. It would be an apt final chapter to the NID story, which mirrors the wider narrative of electronic music's trajectory within South Asia, a disparate timeline with moments of activity interspersed within silence, that when stitched together across decades reveals a fractured yet subtly determinable continuum. It is a hope that as further research comes to light in the field of electronic sound in South Asia and additional archives are uncovered that more points in this timeline will be plotted together, slowly giving greater clarity to this elusive map, forefronting unheard stories and forgotten voices who await rediscovery, and shedding new light on the lost pioneers of sound from the subcontinent.

Notes

1   Samit Das, *Architecture of Santiniketan, Tagore's Concept of Space*, Chapter 2.

2   G. Geethika, 'Learning by Doing': Understanding the Gandhian Approach to Education' in *Journal of Polity & Society* (2021).

3   Swati Gosh, *Design Movements in Tagore's Santiniketan*, Preface.

4   Letter from Douglas Ensminger to JDR 3rd on December 10, 1954, in RG 5, Box 45, Folder 413, Asian Interests, India, 1954–1955.

5   Michael Warner, 'Origins of the Congress for Cultural Freedom, 1949–1950', CIA In-house journal, 2007.

6   Harm Langenkamp, *"A Most Interesting and Complex Involvement": Cold War Alignments between the Ford and Rockefeller Foundations, the Congress for Cultural Freedom, and the Central Intelligence Agency*, Utrecht University (2021).

7   Saloni Mathur, 'Charles and Ray Eames in India' in *Art Journal* vol. 70, no. 1 (Spring 2011).

8   MoMA Archives, *Design Today in America and Europe*. PDF Catalogue—ICIP_I-B-224.pdf.

9   Julie Martin with Jared Bark and Anna Lundh, NID Ahmedabad CMR, https://www.youtube.com/@nationalinstituteofdesigna197.

10   Vikram Sarbhai, Quotation of the Day, https://www.tribuneindia.com.

11   Interview Alexander Keefe, Delhi India, Feb 2022, BBC Radio 3.

12   'Expo '70 as Watershed: The Politics of American Art and Technology' in *Cold War Modern: Design 1945–1970*, V&A Publishing.

13   Atul Desai, NID composers interview, All India Radio 1970—NID Tape Archives

14   Shilpa Das, 'The Moog Synthesizer: Electronic Music and a Design Institute in India' in Paul Purgas (ed.), *Subcontinental Synthesis*, Strange Attractor Press.

15   Voyager Golden Record—https://en.wikipedia.org/wiki/Voyager_Golden_Record.

16   https://www.thewire.co.uk/in-writing/interviews/can-we-float-in-the-air-an-interview-with-eat-s-julie-martin.

17   Intro scene from *The Alien* script, an unmade film by Satyajit Ray—Travails with the Alien: The Film That Was Never Made and Other Adventures with Science Fiction 18 'Building on a Prehistory: Artists' Film and New Media in India, Part 2'—https://lux.org.uk.

19   Suparno Banerjee, *Indian Science Fiction: Patterns, History and Hybridity*, University of Wales Press.

20   'Lunar tunes: How Music Responded to the Era of Space Travel'—https://www.ft.com/content/57e2b32c-a49c-11e9-974c-ad1c6ab5efd1.

21   'Sputnik I: The Beeps Heard Round The World'—https://www.hoover.org/research/sputnik-i-beeps-heard-round-world.

22   Charles & Ray Eames, The India Report, 1958—http://echo.iat.sfu.ca/library/eames_58_india_report.pdf.

23   Sandhya Desai in an online interview with Shilpa Das, February 10, 2022.

24   E.A.T. Archives—Moderna Museet Stockholm.

25   'No Free Launch: Designing the Indian National Satellite'—https://history.nasa.gov/SP-4217/ch16.htm.

26   Henry Kissinger, *The Anderson Papers*—Washington Special Action Group secret meeting transcript, Dec 1971.

27   Virender Kumar, 'Indo-US Cooperation in Civil Space'—www.nasa.gov.

28   Email correspondence interview with Shrinand Desai (Son of Atul Desai), 10th February 2021.

Image Credits

Cover
Tape and voiceover work at the NID sound studio circa 1969.
(National Institute of Design-Archive, Ahmedabad)

Foreword
Rabindranath Tagore making an early voice recording 1921
(bpk / Deutsches Historisches Museum)

Shilpa Das
1 Akhil Succena assessing slides at the NID circa 1970
(National Institute of Design-Archive, Ahmedabad)
2 (L-R) Hasu Qureshi, Akhil Succena, Amritlal Kalal and S.C. Sharma in the sound studio circa 1970.
(National Institute of Design-Archive, Ahmedabad)
3 David Tudor with S.C. Sharma in Ahmedabad 1969
(National Institute of Design-Archive, Ahmedabad)

You Nakai
David Tudor teaching at NID 1969
(National Institute of Design-Archive, Ahmedabad)
Fig 01 Letter from Sarabhai Agencies to David Tudor 1968
(You Nakai)
Fig 02 Extended Voices compilation record (You Nakai)

Fig 03 Overview of NID Moog Modules (You Nakai)
Fig 04 David Tudor equipment list for India (You Nakai)
Fig 05 David Tudor equipment list for India (You Nakai)
Fig 06 David Tudor teaching at NID 1969
(National Institute of Design-Archive, Ahmedabad)

Geeta Dayal
Suresh Shottam of The Spartans. Bristol Beat Contest, Bengaluru, 1968.

Alannah Chance
Gautum Gira Sarabhai Square at the NID campus
(Kill joyarchivist CC 4.0 via Wikimedia Commons)

Jinraj Joshipura
1 Voice recording at the NID sound studio circa 1970
(National Institute of Design-Archive, Ahmedabad)
2 Jinraj Joshupura portrait (Jinraj Joshipura)
3 Synthesizer 'sheet music' by Jinraj Joshpura 1969 (Jinraj Joshipura)
4 Live concert sketch 1972 (Jinraj Joshipura)
5 Inflatable interactive sound tunnel at NID circa 1969
(National Institute of Design-Archive, Ahmedabad)

6 Sketch of stage design by Jinraj Joshipura 1972 (Jinraj Joshipura)

Rahila Haque
1 Portrait of Gita Sarabhai, 1951 (Nathan Hughes Hamilton, CC BY 2.0 via Wikimedia Commons)
2 Jiddu Krishnamurti in Vienna 1923 (Krishnamurti Foundation Trust)
3 Tape 445 from the NID archives produced by Gita Sarabhai (Paul Purgas)
4 David Tudor and Gita Sarabhai in Ahmedabad 1969 (National Institute of Design-Archive, Ahmedabad)

Matt Williams
1 Architectural site plan of the NID campus (National Institute of Design-Archive, Ahmedabad)
2 NID campus entrance area (Shutterstock)
3 Sanskar Kendra Museum in Ahmedabad, designed by Le Corbusier (AgeFotostock)
4 Villa de Madame Manorama Sarabhai, designed by Le Corbusier (Alamy)

Paul Purgas
1 Dome of the Indian Pavilion at the Osaka Expo 1970 (RIBApix)
2 I.S. Mathur & Atul Desai working in the NID studio circa 1970 (Shrinand Desai)

3 Bob Moog and team with the NID synthesizer crated for transit (Roger Luther MoogArchives.com)
4 Tape 439 interior reference notes (Paul Purgas)

Index

Strange Attractor Press 2024